THE
Many Loves of Parenting

Thomas & Nanette KINKADE

with LARRY LIBBY

THE Many Loves of Parenting

Multnomah Publishers *Sisters, Oregon*

THE MANY LOVES OF PARENTING
published by Multnomah Publishers, Inc.
Text © 2003 by Thomas and Nanette Kinkade
Featuring artwork by Thomas Kinkade © 2003 by Thomas Kinkade,
Media Arts Group, Inc., Morgan Hill, CA
International Standard Book Number: 1-59052-088-2

Design by Koechel Peterson & Associates, Inc., Minneapolis, Minnesota

Unless otherwise indicated, Scripture quotations are from:
The Holy Bible, New International Version
© 1973, 1984 by International Bible Society,
used by permission of Zondervan Publishing House.
All rights reserved

Other Scripture quotations are from:
Holy Bible, New Living Translation (NLT)
© 1996. Used by permission of Tyndale House Publishers, Inc.
All rights reserved.

The Modern Language Bible (MLB)
© 1945, 1959, © 1969 by the Zondervan Publishing House.
Old Testament Section, Copyright
© 1959 by the Zondervan Publishing House.
All Rights Reserved Including that of Translation.

New American Standard Bible (NASB)
© 1960, 1977 by the Lockman Foundation

Multnomah is a trademark of Multnomah Publishers, Inc.,
and is registered in the U.S. Patent and Trademark Office.
The colophon is a trademark of Multnomah Publishers, Inc.

Printed in the United States of America

For information:
MULTNOMAH PUBLISHERS, INC.
POST OFFICE BOX 1720
SISTERS, OREGON 97759

Library of Congress Cataloging-in-Publication Data
Kinkade, Thomas, 1958-
    The many loves of parenting / by Thomas & Nanette Kinkade.
        p. cm.
ISBN 1-59052-088-2
1. Parenting—Religious aspects—Christianity. I. Kinkade, Nanette. II. Title.
    BV4529 .K56 2003
    248.8'4—dc21

                        2002153213
        03 04 05 06 07 08 09—10 9 8 7 6 5 4 3 2 1 0

Contents

What If....?

Just for fun, just for a moment, let's do a little "what if" thinking.

What if…we decided to make the development of our children and the strengthening of our family the most important things (next to our relationship with God and our spouse) in all of life?

What if…we took strong and deliberate steps to strengthen the "home and family" components of daily living?

What if…in doing so, we ended up going straight against the current of popular culture, to the point that others considered our commitments overboard or excessive?

What if…we cared more about the character and future well-being of our children than what everybody in the whole world thought about our honest, heartfelt efforts?

What if…before God, we poured our love, our time, our creativity, and our very life energies into this task we call parenting?

What would life be like?

A Vigilant

CHAPTER ONE

Love

Thomas Kinkade

So then, let us not be like others,

who are asleep, but let us be alert.

1 Thessalonians 5:6

IMAGINE YOURSELF A RESIDENT OF SOME SMALL BANANA REPUBLIC.

When you think about it, every day in the life of a child is a revolution.

You go to bed one night with an iron-fisted authoritarian government gripping the reins of power. You wake up the next morning to hear that a revolution has taken place. The old regime has been swept away. The former dictators are on the run. A new president is on television, making a speech, declaring new elections. Crowds gather in the streets, life has changed overnight, and new flags fly from ten thousand flagpoles.

Some such upheavals change things for the better, some for the worse. The only thing you can be sure about is that revolutions make for uncertain times and uncertain results. They may mean liberation. They may mean slavery. They may usher in a season of prosperity and joy. They may open the door to years of sorrow.

It makes good sense to be vigilant in the middle of a revolution. Stay flexible. Be wary. Keep in touch with the march of events. And keep your eyes open all the time.

When you think about it, *every day* in the life of a child is a revolution.

Every day, the world changes.

Every day, life reinvents itself.

Children absorb knowledge and experiences at an astonishing rate. Just think of a newborn baby, whose awareness of his world probably doubles every waking hour. Or consider a wide-eyed five-year-old, drinking in her surroundings in great gulps.

These mini-revolutions may be silent or loud. Peaceful or violent. Helpful or destructive. They may come in a great rush, like floodwater gushing through a broken levee, or drip by drip, like droplets wearing away stone. Whether you are the parent of a toddler, a cheerful nine-year-old, or a sometimes-turbulent adolescent, life is a *kaleidoscope* of physical transformation, ceaseless learning, spiritual seeking, and social adjustment.

A kaleidoscope?

Have you ever peered through one of those strange telescopic-looking devices? Some are little more than cheap toys. Others are highly elaborate, finely crafted instruments—creations of crystal and teak—that can run into the thousands of dollars.

No matter what you pay for the privilege, gazing into a light source through a kaleidoscope can be a fascinating experience. One tiny turn of the ring, and the whole scene alters before your eyes. New, startling patterns flower in an instant. Old designs change in a blink, never to return.

If raising children is like looking through a kaleidoscope, what does that say about the role of a parent?

You have to be alert. You have to be vigilant. You have to remember that tomorrow may look nothing like today. And you have to depend on the Lord—daily, hourly—for wisdom.

You have to be alert. You have to be vigilant. You have to remember that tomorrow may look nothing like today.

First and foremost, God has given you the high honor and privilege of guiding those daily revolutions in the life of your child. Of *being there* through many of those changes, transformations, and transmutations.

To put it plainly, parents simply can't afford to be long off the scene.

Or self-absorbed.

Or distracted and absentminded.

Or politically correct and committed to every cause but that of raising their own children.

If they are, they will surrender irretrievable opportunities to teach, model, offer course corrections, deal with negative, invasive attitudes and actions, and create positive first impressions.

As someone has well said, "Home is where life makes up its mind."

Nanette: ❧

*W*e've just experienced one of those mini-revolutions with our thirteen-year-old.

Since she was tiny, Merritt has always been interested in animals and sports and all kinds of outdoor activities. A confirmed tomboy! She detested the color pink, and whenever I tried to dress the girls in frilly little matching dresses (as I so love to do), it was not a happy occasion for Merritt. How can you play soccer or climb a tree in all that lace and finery?

Disappointed as we might have been at certain moments, Thomas and I allowed Merritt to be herself and (within limits) to dress as she wished. Yes, there were times when we insisted on appropriate, feminine attire, but her outfit of choice was baggy overalls—and her afternoon activities revolved around playing sports (mostly with the boys).

And then came the revolution.

The day after her thirteenth birthday, everything changed. The reality came home to me on our first shopping trip after her birthday party. Her new school was having a get-together, and she wanted "something new" to wear. I have to admit, I found myself thinking, *But you already have six pairs of overalls!* Instead, she went right to the rack and picked out a skirt.

A skirt?

A pink skirt.

Pink?

And then she picked out a little pink blouse with delicate, puffy sleeves. With great difficulty, I restrained my reaction. "Oh, that's cute, Merritt. *Very* nice."

The revolution has continued apace. Her taste in clothing has rapidly evolved from denim and sneakers to anything cute and frilly. Now she's into experimenting with hairstyles and a little makeup. And when you go into her room and look in her closet, guess what color is everywhere?

Pink in every shade.

While she still enjoys animals and sports, Merritt has now discovered the telephone, dressing up to look feminine, and being with her girlfriends every possible moment she can. (And this is only teenage daughter number one!)

My point is that these changes arrived *almost overnight.* If I had been on a two-day business trip of some kind, I would have returned to find a different girl living under the Kinkade roof.

A vigilant love draws its energy, awareness, and perspective from a daily walk with the Lord.

But in some sense, that is true every day in our home. The kaleidoscope keeps changing—not just with Merritt, but with all four girls. That's our family dynamic, and I imagine most families experience something similar. I've never raised a boy, but I can report that with four daughters, emotions rush through the house like criss-crossing streams. Laughter. Tears. Anger. Indignation. Joy. Melancholy. Tenderness. Delight.

It's an exciting place to be for a mom and homemaker.

But there is no way I could even pretend to stay on top of things in my own strength and wisdom. A vigilant love draws its energy, awareness, and perspective from a daily walk with the Lord.

I recently came across these words of Jesus as I was reading the book of John:

"I am the vine; you are the branches. If a man remains in me and I in him, he will bear much fruit; apart from me you can do nothing." (15:5)

I couldn't help but think of parenting, and all those daily, hourly kaleidoscope changes. The longer I am a mom, the more I realize how completely dependent I am upon the Lord. Of course, this is true with every believer and every issue in life, but I especially sense my need to lean on Jesus as a parent. Raising children is such a fast-moving, ever-changing scene that you have to keep Him central—or get blown away!

I've made a habit of starting every morning in prayer, seeking the Lord's covering and protection for my

> *Raising children is such a fast-moving, ever-changing scene that you have to keep Him central— or get blown away!*

daughters, asking that His hand might rest upon each one of their lives, guiding them moment by moment. Before I get up from my knees, I ask the Lord to just brace me for the changes and challenges of the day.

Scripture asks the question, "How do you know what will happen tomorrow?" (James 4:14, NLT). The answer, of course, is that we don't. We can't know what will happen even one minute from now.

The fact is, every day is a revolution, and I don't want to be caught napping. ✍

Each child in our home is in reality *many* children.

Our task as parents is to adjust and respond to a child who will wear a hundred—maybe a thousand—faces through the years. What we're talking about is at least an eighteen-year assignment, with an incredible diversity of experience within that role and position.

I'm reminded of starting a business. There are things you attend to at the start-up phase—laying the physical groundwork, developing a vision statement, infrastructure, plans, an organizational chart. These are launch points. Baby steps. But as

the business grows, its needs rapidly change. Old assumptions land in the dumpster as you hammer out new working plans in the heat and pressure of marketplace realities. Every passing day presses and presses you toward further fine-tuning and sophistication.

Perhaps for a few years you served as founder and manager of the whole operation, but then one day you wake up and realize that you're in charge of an international business that has just about outpaced its infrastructure. How will you respond? Or will you respond at all? Unless you transform yourself into a new leader for the new business you have...the enterprise will perish.

Our task as parents is to adjust and respond to a child who will wear a hundred faces through the years.

The same is true for parents. Parenting a little baby is a very different proposition from parenting a toddler. The parent of a ten-year-old discovers a whole new set of issues different from the parent of a kindergartener. The parent of a teen is suddenly in strange, new territory, as Nanette and I are finding out. When our children become young adults, or parents in their own right, the relationship and expectations will change yet again.

The kaleidoscope turns, the patterns change, and you move all too rapidly into a new reality. And another. And another.

God helping me, I don't want to miss any of those phases,

any of those mini-revolutions. (Who knows which one might mark my child's character for the rest of her life?) I want to be the dad my girls need, when they need him. I happen to believe that this is one of the chief reasons God placed me on this planet.

In essence, of course, every child needs certain basics: security, safety, shelter, love, affirmation, and nutrition. But within those unchanging foundational needs, the world alters dramatically every month, every week, sometimes every day.

At times you will hear moms or dads say, "I don't know what happened. It's like I don't even know my son any-more. I looked across the room at him the other day and felt like I was looking at a stranger. I have no idea what's going on in his heart these days."

One turn of the kaleidoscope and everything looks different.

It can happen! One turn of the kaleidoscope and everything looks different. That's the reason to stay awake, to stay alert, to stay on task, and to stay in touch with your child as much as you possibly can.

CATCHING TRENDS EARLY

Not long after Merritt had linked up with a new group of girls at school, Nanette and I began to notice a few changes. Nothing major. Nothing earthshaking. And yet...it was becoming obvious the kaleidoscope had turned, and some-thing seemed different.

It began with a seeming loss of appetite. She would sit down at the table and take tiny portions, sometimes not even finishing those. This wasn't our old Merritt! And yet she kept saying she "just wasn't hungry."

After a couple weeks of this, it dawned on us that she was basically starving herself. As we began to probe a little, we discovered that all her friends in this new little peer group were thin as pencils—and almost seemed to worship thinness. Anxious to be accepted with this newest circle of friends, Merritt reasoned that she wouldn't fit in unless she became as thin as they were.

In God's grace and kindness, she grew through that stage and got over it after about a year. Nanette and I spent a lot of time with her, encouraging and affirming her, explaining how some people place an unhealthy emphasis on their weight. In time, Merritt leveled out to some healthy eating habits and a healthy body type.

But it was sobering to us. What if Nanette and I had been preoccupied? What if we had been absorbed in our business enterprises, or in our media interviews, or running in a thousand different directions, and hadn't noticed? *What if we hadn't intercepted this trend in time?*

Some revolutions need to be stopped in their tracks.

Nanette:

Since Thomas and I are both very concerned about our children and stay involved in their daily lives, we've been able to discuss serious issues like these and put together a game plan as a team. Together, we'll sit down and talk about the issue with our daughters. More than once, we've seen what could have been very negative trends redirected and turned in a positive direction.

I think it would be safe to say that only involved, vigilant parents have that opportunity.

Once again, it's an area for prayer. We pray continually that the Lord will keep us aware, keep us sensitive, keep us alert and tuned in to the issues in our daughters' lives. As in so many matters of the heart, we're completely dependent on His Spirit and His wisdom. As close as we may be to our children, only God knows their inmost thoughts, their unspoken fears, their secret dreams.

The apostle Paul speaks about developing "eyes of the heart," eyes that see deeper than the surface of things. That's what I pray for Thom and myself as parents.

With the kind of business and media pressures Thom and I face every day, we have to work very hard not to become too caught up in this interview deadline or that "new opportunity"—and become less available to our children. Though I recognize it's not possible for everyone, I've thanked the Lord many times that we're in a position where I can be at home full time and intimately involved in our children's lives.

As close as we may be to our children, only God knows their inmost thoughts, their unspoken fears, their secret dreams.

You might think that as the children grow older, the need for involvement and vigilance would gradually scale back. But that's not so! I believe it needs to continue at much the same intensity as when they were small. Yes, it's a different type of involvement and focus, but it still needs to be there at full strength! The issues may vary from year to year, but they remain very, very critical issues.

In our home, Thom and I have decided to limit access to media coming through our doors. We've never had commercial television. We take no newspapers or newsmagazines. Our main telephone is in my office, in the center of our home. The computer is there, too, and everyone understands that its use is limited to schoolwork and special projects. Because she is so social, Merritt is allowed fifteen minutes of "chat time" with her friends on the Internet each night. But it all takes place in the center of the home and the heart of family life and activities.

So much of vigilance as a parent is a *time* issue. How can you possibly know what's going on in the lives of your children, how can you begin to grasp what they are thinking, feeling, and becoming if you aren't investing your time in them? Without those significant blocks of time together every day, how will you know how the kaleidoscope has changed? You won't notice the subtle changes in attitude, in facial expressions, in habits, in friends, or in hobbies, interests, and music. You won't see those things as they begin to change, you won't pick up on what's going on, and you will have lost your opportunity for input or correction.

If you're becoming weary as a parent, the easy path is to simply "back off" and allow your child to bond completely with his or her peer group. *After all, isn't that what teenagers do? Wouldn't it be easier to put a phone in her room, to put the Internet in her room, and get her out of my hair? She could talk on the phone all evening or chat on-line. She'd be happy, and things might be a little more peaceful.* Out of convenience, then, you would not only be choosing to link your child with her peers; you would also be choosing to cut her off from family influence and family interaction.

So much of vigilance as a parent is a time issue.

There's no doubt about it, creating strong links with the family requires a great deal more energy, time, thought, patience, and creativity than buckling under to a teen's desire to follow the crowd.

Merritt, of course, *wanted* a phone in her own room. We thought about it...but then concluded, "If she had a phone in her room, our family times together would be out the window. We wouldn't see her anymore. Her sisters wouldn't see her anymore. And that's just too big a price to pay."

So the Kinkades still have one main phone for everybody. It has a cord on it, just like phones used to have in the old days. And it doesn't allow anyone to divide themselves off from the rest of the family.

We have a strict "no phone policy" at mealtimes. No one, from Thomas to little Evie, gets up from the table to take calls. The dinner hour is sacred territory at the Kinkade home. After 8:30 we let the answering machine pick up our calls. This is a time when the house is beginning to calm and quiet down, perhaps after a hectic day, and we do our best to preserve a peaceful environment, where we can read and converse with one another without the intrusions and distractions of the outside world.

The dinner hour is the heart of our day together as a family.

28

Nanette: THE HEART OF OUR DAY

The dinner hour is the heart of our day together as a family. As we finish the meal, we go around the table and each of us shares a prayer need in our lives or something for which we are especially thankful.

This has turned out to be the perfect time for our family sharing. We're all together, we've all eaten, and (hopefully) everyone is relaxed and in a good mood. So we can really give the Lord praise together and pray about whatever needs have surfaced during the day. For instance, one of the girl's teacher's husband has cancer; we've been praying for him every night. Or maybe one of their friends is struggling with some nagging problem or decision.

It's been so exciting as a family to see the Lord's answers—in so many situations. As we've witnessed the Lord work time after time, we've been encouraged to share more and more requests with each other.

But this family prayer time has another very strong benefit for Thom and me. Through the requests and the prayers, we're able to better understand and keep up with what most concerns each of our girls on a nightly basis.

We learn what they're thinking about, what they're bubbling over to share, and what weighs on their hearts. It opens our eyes to areas that need special nurturing or empathy. Even silence or downcast eyes during our sharing time can alert us to changing situations and opportunities for parenting-in-private.

That's why we've made dinnertime so sacred in our home. That's why we refuse to allow other activities or commitments to intrude. That's why we won't take calls. This sort of valuable bonding-and-sorting-out time simply couldn't happen if we were bouncing up and down to answer the phone, or racing through traffic from Taco Bell to a church function or to a soccer game.

Even the little ones participate with enthusiasm. Sometimes the prayer requests can be so touching—

> *We learn what they're thinking about, what they're bubbling over to share, and what weighs on their hearts.*

and at other times it's all I can do to keep from laughing out loud!

One recent prayer concern involved one of our two Jack Russell terriers. The male, "Junior," is a little go-getter, always sticking his nose where it doesn't belong. On one recent romp in the country, he stuck his nose down a hole—and was bitten by a rattlesnake!

Poor Junior almost didn't emerge from that encounter. He swelled up to un-terrier-like proportions and really seemed to be on his last legs. Honestly, Thomas and I were a little worried about the girls, and how they would handle this, because we didn't see how the little guy would survive.

It concerned all of us, of course, but it was four-year-old Evie's prayer that everyone remembers.

"And, dear Lord," she prayed so sweetly, "please help Junior not to look like a hippopotamus."

That, of course, broke up the prayer time with laughter. Evie, ever delighted to have an audience, laughed, too.

Amazingly, Junior truly did pull through—when there's no way he should have survived. But God was faithful, and Evie got her miracle. These are the sorts of little things—and not so little things—when the kids get to see God work in our lives, and it builds the faith of us all.

Vigilance has a price tag. But the return on the investment makes it all worthwhile.

Because of the demands of Thomas's business, keeping this hour set apart has been very difficult at times. In fact, we just recently went through an evaluation time as a couple and decided that—no matter what, no matter how awkward or difficult, no matter what pressures were induced by whomever—we simply had to cut back on our outside commitments. We had to honestly admit to one another that if we didn't do that, if we kept going the way we had been going, we would begin to miss out on meeting our girls' needs. It was no use fooling ourselves, and we would certainly pay a price we didn't want to pay.

Vigilance has a price tag, too.

But the return on the investment makes it all worthwhile.

Jesus said,
"Let the little children
come to me, and do not
hinder them, for the
kingdom of heaven
belongs to such as these."

MATTHEW 19:14

A Focused

CHAPTER TWO

Love

Thomas Kinkade

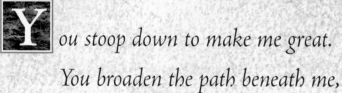

You stoop down to make me great.

You broaden the path beneath me,

so that my ankles do not turn.

PSALM 18:35–36

THERE IS AN APPRECIABLE DIFFERENCE BETWEEN A FLOODLIGHT AND A SPOTLIGHT.

Floodlights drench an area with a wide, milky diffusion, approximating weak daylight. But a spotlight is *focused*, enveloping and illuminating a single space, a single object...or a single soul.

We appreciate the wide, general flow of light that allows us to find our way and move from place to place in the surrounding darkness.

But everybody needs a little time in the spotlight.

Each child needs to have uninterrupted time with a parent, time when he feels heard, understood, valued, and loved.

Even in a generally happy home (with lots of light and abundant love), a child needs individualized, focused attention. He needs time in that small circle of illumination. He needs time with each parent— to bond, to play, to laugh, to cuddle, to learn, to dream. And as the opportunity presents itself, to discuss the issues of life and eternity.

Obviously, focused love will look different at different ages: For a toddler it may be extra playtime down on the floor with Mom or Dad; for a teenager it may be a "date," going out for a breakfast or lunch with a parent. You might sum it up with a statement like this: Each child needs to have uninterrupted time with a parent, time when he feels heard, understood, valued, and loved.

Just think back. Can you remember those times as a child when you longed to have Mom or Dad to yourself for a while? Can you recall wishing for just a little bit of time in the spot-light of attention and love?

Because my studio is just next door to our house, I like to take a break from my painting in the afternoon and walk over to see what's happening on the home front. If one of the kids is out playing in the yard or shooting baskets, I'll stop—for a few minutes at least—and make contact.

In the time that I have, I try to seek out each of my daughters. I don't just assume they're self-occupied and content.

I might begin by tracking down each of the little ones. Where are they? *"Oh, they're downstairs playing a game."* So I sit down to watch...or maybe join in the fun for a few minutes.

Where are the older ones? *Merritt's on the phone, and Chandler's doing homework."*

At the very least, I will make eye contact and put my hand on each of them. If one is on the phone, I'll touch her on the arm or shoulder. Just to make contact. Just to bridge whatever dis-tance there might be in the relationship. I'll say, "How ya doin', honey?" And she may put her hand over the mouthpiece of the phone and say, "Oh, hi, Dad."

Sometimes it's necessary to bend down to their level. If they're sitting down, I'll try to sit down right beside them. And what does that communicate? That I have stopped what I am doing, that I've set aside my world—if only for a few choice moments—to enter theirs.

It's a simple way of showing that I'm *with* them.

I am there.

I am available.

I am at their level.

I delight in their company.

I relish their presence.

I'm not just towering over them as the authority figure; I'm also there beside them in an intimate and personal way.

To me, it's a picture of the way the Lord Jesus relates to each of us. He is the ultimate Authority, not only over each life, but over the whole universe. And yet He stoops down to be with us right at our level. In awe of this thought, David once wrote, "You stoop down to make me great" (Psalm 18:35). In the ultimate stooping, the Almighty was born as a baby on this small planet, becoming Emmanuel, *God with Us*. This is a God who will never, never remain aloof when one of His children is going through pain, difficulty, or sorrow. The Bible affirms that "the LORD is close to the brokenhearted; he rescues those who are crushed in spirit" (Psalm 34:18, NLT).

In Psalm 40, David tells how the Lord *inclined* to him, or turned to him, in a moment of deep trouble. He writes:

He inclined to me and heard my cry.
He brought me up out of the pit of
*   destruction, out of the miry clay,*
And He set my feet upon a rock making
*   my footsteps firm.*
(PSALM 40:1–2, NASB)

> *I'm not just towering over them as the authority figure; I'm also there beside them in an intimate and personal way.*

No one seems to be quite sure what that Hebrew word translated *inclined* means. But I can picture David pulling on the Lord's robe, saying, "Lord, help! I'm in trouble down here. Bend over to hear me. Come down to help me out of this terrible place. Be with me, Lord! Stoop down. You're awfully big, and I'm awfully small. Would You just bend over to see things from my point of view for a moment?"

Sometimes I think we make this parenting business sound more complicated and intimidating than it really needs to be. Prospective parents sometimes imagine they'll have to become some supercharged, ultra-wise combination of drill sergeant, youth pastor, child psychologist, and pediatrician. Because each of my girls has a unique personality, for instance, some might say I have to find some elaborate, specialized key to unlock the heart of each child.

It's really not that complex. All four of my daughters—and Nanette, too, for that matter—need the same thing from me.

Time.

My time. My attention. My listening ear. My availability. My compassion. My hand to cling to. My shoulder to cry on.

> *We're together, doing something we love. And that is powerful.*

What they are looking for is really not that much different than what David sought. They need someone to incline to them, someone to step down a little and get close, someone to hear them, someone to climb down off the throne and out of the exalted regions of the adult world to just *be* with them. Do you realize how simple, uncomplicated, and *unbelievably powerful* that is?

"QUALITY" OR QUANTITY?

Now, what I actually do with each child may vary a great deal because they have different interests, enjoy different sports, pursue different hobbies, and look forward to different activities. But whatever the activity, whatever the venue, I try to find something special to do with each child several times a week.

Little Winsor, for example, loves to draw. So I'll say, "Winsor, why don't you come over to my studio while I'm working, and you can draw some pictures while I paint." I'll set her up with a little space, and she'll content herself with her colored pencils for longer than you might imagine a seven-year-old could sit still. I get absorbed in my painting, and she gets absorbed in her drawing, but we're in the same room together and we treasure each other's company.

We have proximity.

We're together, doing something we love.

And that is powerful.

She'll bring her picture over to me from time to time and show me what she's working on, and I'll have the opportunity to affirm her. She will look over my shoulder at my efforts, and I'll try to explain my plan and goal for the painting. It's a very meaningful time for both of us.

But it wouldn't work at all with Merritt, my oldest.

She has no interest in sitting still, much less in "quietly communing." She likes rapid-fire conversation and lots of action! So I'll say, "Hey, let's go out and shoot some hoops—one-on-one!" We'll keep a constant banter going as we bump and harass and guard one another. I get in her face, and she gets in mine. Merritt loves that. For her, that's proximity and closeness.

Chandler has a diversity of interests, but tends to be one who wants to talk about school, or read us her homework assignments. From day one of kindergarten, it seems, she's been a

motivated, committed student. She really *likes* doing homework. And it's unbelievably affirming to her when we show interest in her studies and work with her and affirm her a little as she tackles her assignments. That makes her feel loved, and we love the special time with her.

So which is most important, quality time or quantity time?

I vote for quantity.

Why? Because quality *grows out of* quantity, not the other way around. You can't force happiness or deep conversations or crazy memories. You can't program the insights and bonding that arise out of relaxed, unstructured time with the family. It is within a quantity of time that small moments of quality time occur. It doesn't work to say, "Okay, kids, get ready. We're going to have quality time on Tuesday night from seven to eight." Those truly unforgettable, golden moments in any relationship occur as people are together for a long time, simply enjoying one another's company in a relaxed, safe, unhurried setting.

> *It is within a quantity of time that small moments of quality time occur.*

DIVIDE AND CONQUER

For Nanette and me, the "divide and conquer" method has become a vital element of our parenting style. Having all four of the girls together all the time certainly isn't best for any of us. Each girl wants something more than a "group identity," and who can blame her?

So every now and then we will break them up into smaller groups and different combinations. Sometimes I'll take the little ones and do something fun with them while Nanette goes shopping with the older girls. Then we'll swap and do it the other way around.

Just last Sunday, after church, I decided to take the two youngest Kinkades in tow. As we came out into the parking lot on a beautiful California morning, I said, "Nanette, if you wouldn't mind, I'm going to take these two little girls and we'll just walk home from church in this pretty sunshine. And, oh (with a wink to the little ones), we just *may* stop for lunch at the Hamburger Stand."

By simply taking the opportunity to step out of the rut... we grabbed a lasting memory by the tail.

Far from minding, Nanette smiled sweetly at her good fortune. Evie and Winsor had been a little sleep deprived the night before—and cranky all morning as a result.

"Okay, girls," I said, "let's get out and get some exercise."

To tell the truth, I underestimated how far two miles can be when you're walking in the hot sunshine at a little girl's pace. We got our exercise, all right—and then some. I also hadn't counted on the fact that I would end up *carrying* one of them about half the distance.

But nobody was in a particular hurry that day, and we managed tolerably well. We stopped for a Slurpee at the 7-Eleven on the corner. We ate cheeseburgers and French fries at our beloved Hamburger Stand. Then we found a "shortcut" through the neighborhoods up in the hills and wandered around a bit trying to find our way home again. (We were never actually lost, just temporarily misplaced.)

All in all, it was a most successful enterprise—and one that Thomas Kinkade will never forget. By simply taking the opportunity to step out of the rut and do something different with the kids, we grabbed a lasting memory by the tail—and savored an hour or two of comradely adventure.

At other times, Nanette will have three of the girls and I'll be one-on-one with the other. Maybe it will be just Dad and Merritt, taking a walk and getting an ice cream cone...or Mom and Evie, playing on the swings and slide (and maybe eating a little picnic) at a local park.

As I've said, it really isn't rocket science.

It's just a willingness to spend time with your children. To sacrifice other priorities, other responsibilities, and other diversions in order to invest your life in them.

As a result, no one feels jealous or left out because one of the girls gets special time with Dad or Mom. Each of them knows that her time will come, too.

And it does.

Nanette: 🌿

*I*t's so amazing to me how the family dynamic changes when even one of the children is away at some activity. The usual alliances shift around, and new ones form. It's good for all of us to mix and match our family groupings from time to time.

But there is nothing like one-on-one.

As Thomas has said, we all need a little time in the spotlight of focused love and attention.

All children go through times of struggle, when they're feeling a little more emotional or insecure. Not long ago I noticed this with Chandler, our second daughter. At the time, I'd been reading a Christian book that was a particular blessing to me. It was just a simple, positive little message that talked about having an attitude of praise and thanks and really getting your eyes back on the Lord. It was a fun read and whimsically illustrated, so I thought it might be something that Chandler would enjoy. I asked her if she would like to read it with me, and she said she would.

We began to carve out some time together every night. After we put the little ones to bed and Merritt was busy with homework, we would take a little time to just snuggle close on the couch and read together.

What a good time that was with my Chandler! We had those few nights to enjoy some special closeness and to read some positive and uplift-ing material together. The Lord had made me sensitive to the fact that she needed that little bit of extra time—and it was encouraging for me, too.

We all need a little time in the spotlight of focused love and attention.

With the younger ones, of course, there has to be time for play.

I'll take one or both of them to a nearby park for a

morning or afternoon of play and laughter, chatter and cuddle time.

The older girls love our shopping dates! I can almost always be persuaded (twist my arm!) to hit the malls, but what makes it truly special is just having that private time to talk and share together along the way. And (believe it or not) it's not so much what we are going out to buy; it's having that one-on-one mother-daughter time with one another.

> *I can always tell the difference when one of the girls comes home from time with her dad.*

Thom's been great about doing this, too. He'll take the girls on little dates—and even an occasional overnighter. Maybe they'll go out hiking or horseback riding and just "hang out" together on a weekend. I can always tell the difference when one of the girls comes home from a time like that with her dad. It bolsters her self-image, and she looks refreshed and happy.

With a little time in the spotlight of focused love, it seems like all the shadows and cares just melt away.

It's true for little people...and big ones, too.

Nanette: ❧ PASSING ON THE LEGACY

When I was in high school, my dad and I started a habit of jogging together every morning. Six o'clock would come around, and I'd hear Dad making his usual obnoxious whistling noise at my door. It became a running joke between us because it was such an aggravating sound. But it definitely got me up out of bed.

We'd lace up our sneakers and jog over to the local high school track. In the next half hour, we'd run about three miles...and talk nonstop. What a wonderful bonding time for Dad and me. There I was, trying to get through high school, with all the changes, excitement, heartaches, and uncertainties. And I had my dad and his listening ear for half an hour every morning through all those years.

Mom and I had time together, too...while shopping (what else?). Because we lived up in the hills in the little town of Placerville, we'd take the half-hour ride down to the valley to shop in Sacramento. And there were no quiet moments on that journey! We would spend the whole time talking about—everything! I considered my mom my best friend—even over any of my girl-friends at school. And looking back, I know the reason why. She was a *faithful* friend. I never had to worry about her gossiping or sharing any of my secrets. She was my confidant and I could trust her completely. She listened and listened and listened to my ramblings.

And I basked all alone in the spotlight of her attention and love.

> *I'm trying to shine the spotlight of my full attention on each of my daughters and allow them to just soak it all in, and never, never doubt my love.*

I often think of that as I try to relate to my own girls. I hope and pray that I've learned some of those listening skills. As parents, we're always ready to dispense advice or solve problems at the drop of a hat. Sometimes it's difficult to get it through my head that my girls don't really want a ton of advice. They mostly just need someone to hear them out. So when I feel compelled to deliver Lecture #77 or drop a dump truck load of wisdom, I've been trying to bite my tongue just a little.

I'm trying to slow down and listen, as my mother and father so patiently listened to me.

I'm trying to shine the spotlight of my full attention on each of my daughters and allow them to just soak it all in, and never, never doubt my love. ◎

My mom was very specific in her parenting style. Her philosophy was pretty simple: unconditional love combined with prayer. There wasn't much emphasis on discipline in our home—although she might have chased after my brother and me with a mop a time or two.

Mom was very loving. She didn't have much physical energy after working all day—I remember her walking in the door almost ready to drop. Even so, she somehow took time to affirm Patrick and me. If we drew something, she would manage to get it framed and hung on the wall. If we shared some crazy idea or wild, implausible dream with her, she would become very animated and say, "Oh! Wouldn't that be *wonderful!*"

She was honestly engaged. She truly listened. And both my brother and I wanted to become achievers in life because we really wanted to impress Mom.

She may have been a single mother in an era when single mothers were rare, but she knew how to put each of us in the spotlight of her love.

A Creative

CHAPTER THREE

Love

Thomas
Kinkade

May you experience the love of Christ,
though it is so great you will never fully
understand it.

EPHESIANS 3:19, NLT

START WITH ANY QUALITY OF GOD. TAKE YOUR PICK.

> *A child's life can so readily become a world of wonder.*

Begin to walk (just a few steps) down that pathway— and find yourself utterly beyond your measure.

Try creativity.

He is its very source. Its bottomless, exhaustless, imponderable First Cause. He is the wellspring for every artist who ever painted...every novelist who ever conceived a world of his own...every musician who ever composed...every poet who ever chased a sonnet through the backstreets of his mind...every engineer who ever pondered a moonlit span over a mighty river, where no bridge had stood before.

The artist's eye of the living God blazes from a trillion suns, glints and shimmers in the mysteries of galaxies beyond counting. He mixes His palette for sunsets racing across the circumference of nameless planets no human eye will ever behold.

His name is Creator.

We humans, formed in His image and likeness, apply God-given creativity in varied and wondrous ways. Sometimes as you read a great old novel, relish a classic movie, eat a gourmet meal in a fine restaurant, pause before some masterpiece in a museum…or watch a woman make a few simple touches that transform a whole room, you find yourself a little awed at the creative potential of the human mind.

Where did it come from? Nowhere but God Himself, whether men and women choose to acknowledge Him or not. Even though we are fallen creatures in a world under the curse of sin, the Master Craftsman has implemented something of His fathomless artist's heart within each of our hearts.

But sometimes it seems a little strange to me…. Even though many of us acknowledge parenting as one of the primary pursuits in all of life, how much creativity do we bring to the process? Why do we content ourselves with old formulas, tired clichés, and lackluster routines when it comes to raising our children? A child's life can so readily become a world of wonder; a little forethought by moms and dads can vastly enhance that sense of fun, delight—and even awe—creating lifelong memories. What a return on such a small investment!

A LUNCH PERIOD TO REMEMBER

I believe in going the extra mile to create memorable experiences for my children.

Sometimes I'll even travel that "extra mile" on a motorcycle.

Not long ago I called Chandler's school, making arrangements to pick her up on my Harley for a lunch date. It made for quite an effect to come roaring into the school parking lot as the bell for lunch period rang. Just between you and me, my bike isn't quite street legal when it comes to the local noise ordinances. It is *very* loud. I've spent a lot of time on it, customizing and dressing it out with a fifties outlaw look. (It's a dead-ringer for Marlon Brando's bike in the movie *The Wild One*.)

> *My daughter and I now have one more memory we can share as long as we live.*

Cruising up to the curb where all the kids were standing, I spotted Chandler. Sweeping her up onto the saddle and plunking an oversized black helmet on her, I blasted off into the sunshine. Chandler told me later that her peers were insanely jealous! *"Aw, no fair! You get to leave school and ride on a motorcycle with your dad!"*

We stopped at a little grill adjoining a doughnut shop with one small outdoor table. I can close my eyes right now and see her in her little school uniform, eyes sparkling and cheeks flushed with adventure. We munched our burgers and fries and chatted the hour away. Then we climbed back on the Harley and zoomed back to school, just in time for her next class.

My point is that I could have easily done this alone. I could have walked out of my studio, drove to one of my favorite lunch spots, and spent a forgettable thirty or forty minutes glancing through a newspaper or just watching the people walk by. But with just a little extra forethought and effort, my daughter and I now have one more memory we can share as long as we live.

IMAGINATION ON A BUDGET

Once again, don't imagine I'm speaking of something exotic, elaborate, or expensive. Walking tours of Ireland or snowmobile treks in the Rockies are rare and wonderful experiences if God provides the means. But we didn't have anything approaching such opportunities when I was growing up in Placerville. Even so, my mother—overworked and harried as she may have been at times—still knew how to make some memories with her boys.

Mom was a fan of old-fashioned country auctions—something of a rarity even in those days. When she was a little girl, she would go to these events with her father—one of the exciting memories of her childhood. Just outside Placerville, the little town of El Dorado had one of the last of the old-time auction houses in our area. From the very first time we went with Mom to a Saturday auction, we had the makings of a new Kinkade family tradition.

Patrick and I loved it! Our '53 Ford F-100 pickup would turn into a dusty, stubbly field beside a huge weathered barn that looked a hundred years old (at least to us boys). Stacked by the auctioneer's platform were boxes and crates of the most remarkable variety of junk, curios, and castoff treasures. Sometimes the auctioneer wouldn't even open the box. He

would call out, "Attention here, ladies and gents, we're going to auction off this whole crate, chock-full of mysterious items, as a surprise package!" It was usually some bizarre menagerie of white elephant stuff, and they would get maybe three or four dollars for the whole thing.

We started working on Mom Friday nights after she came home from work, begging her to take us. "Mom, can we go to the auction tomorrow? *Please?*"

And every now and then (perhaps remembering some childhood memory of her own), a little of the old sparkle would come into her eyes and she would smile and say, "Yes. Let's do it! Let's go to the auction!"

To this day I can remember standing in the warm California sun, scuffing the dust with my sneakers, smelling the warm mustiness of the old barn and becoming wildly excited about the potential marvels and riches in a box of somebody else's forgotten discards.

Beyond this occasional Saturday tradition, several times a year Mom would bundle us in the car for a drive along Highway 49, the "Golden Chain Highway," winding its way through the California gold country. Old 49 connects a delightful succession of tiny, picturesque towns with roots in the mining camps of the 1800s. Coloma... Columbia...Mariposa...Sonora...Angels Camp...Jackson.

Jackson was our usual destination, with its narrow streets,

sagging storefronts, and the weathered headframes of defunct gold mines poking from the hills above into the endless blue of the summer sky.

There was an old hillside park in the town. It was nothing elaborate. The grass was weedy and neglected, and the swing set rusty with age. But the ancient, towering oaks provided leafy shade against the afternoon heat, and there was an old steam locomotive custom-made for little boys to climb on.

Mom would pack some sandwiches, and we'd go there for the afternoon. She would sit on a blanket in the grass and read a book or newspaper, and Pat and I, probably eight or nine at the time, were like two cocker spaniel puppies released from a kennel. When we weren't climbing trees, taking the locomotive on imaginary journeys, or assaulting that venerable swing set, we'd scramble up to the top of the hillside, look out over the town and the brown California hills—and come racing back down again with great, loping strides, breathless with laughter.

When I look back now, our activities with Mom seem as simple as can be. We never went very far, spent very much, or worried about a lot of detailed preparations.

And yet Mom did something very significant for two, young fatherless boys: She provided a platform for our imaginations to soar. We had fun together and treasured up some memories. With a little forethought, parents can use what resources they have and find what works for them. *But the key is to get out there and do it.* Use your imagination! (And yes, in spite of what you may have told yourself for years, God did give you one.) Once you begin to think outside the old lines and parameters a little, you may find yourself becoming addicted to the creative side of parenting.

I spoke about that little park in Jackson. But so many small, neighborhood parks sit empty. That's certainly true in my town, and it also seems to be the case in many of the towns and cities I've visited across the country. And yet these neglected little urban oases can become exciting evening destinations for family adventure—particularly during the long summer twilights. Instead of watching one more boring, cynical television program, get out of the house and into the fresh air and take a relaxed stroll to the nearest neighborhood park. Even doing that *once* as a family could open up a whole new avenue of fun and togetherness.

FINGERPRINTS OF THE CREATOR

Whenever we are out in nature as a family—on one of our many walks, on a horseback ride, or even in the car—Nanette and I try to draw attention to the creativity and handiwork of the Lord. It's more than simply exulting over the "beauty of nature"; it's reminding all of us that we have a great and awesome Creator, worthy of our praise, wonder, and awe.

Nanette may be with the little ones, pointing out the odd shapes of certain clouds, the amazing color combinations in a sunset, or the excitement of seeing a double rainbow. I may chime in with a simple object lesson or two if something along the path inspires me.

I've always believed that part of family bonding means creating an atmosphere of reverence for God. There is no glue that sticks a family closer together than a mutual awareness of the Creator and His workmanship. That's one of the reasons the Kinkades try to seek out nature so much—whether on a trip to the beach or right in our own backyard. I love sitting by a stream with my family, or walking through the fields, or just pausing and looking at a flower garden, pointing out something for them to ponder.

I don't mean something heavy or philosophical—nothing that would feel like a "lecture" (tempted as I may be!). But I really like to stop and say to the kids, "Just imagine! The Lord made each blade of grass just a little differently from every other. And look at these flowers! They come up without anyone telling them to. God just put it all in motion. They push their way up through the dirt and darkness to bloom like this in the sunshine, just because of God's love for us."

These are simple truths, but they draw a family closer because they raise the awareness of God's hand and goodness in our lives. I can't help but think of what Moses taught Israel before they ever set foot in the Promised Land. He said, "These commandments that I give you today are to be upon your hearts. Impress them on your children. Talk about them when you sit at home and when you walk along the road, when you lie down and when you get up" (Deuteronomy 6:6–7).

Sometimes when we are "walking by the way," as the Bible puts it, out in some lovely outdoor showcase of God's handiwork, one of the kids will stop and exclaim, "Oh, this is so *beautiful*. This must be what heaven is like!"

It is fun and awe-inspiring to watch the Lord gently instruct these little ones through us. We have no way of knowing which family trip to the park, which motorcycle ride, which moonrise, which early morning walk through the dewy grass, which fragment of conversation will seep into their memories and pop back up years later. It may not be one of my "profound" object lessons on nature; it may be some offhand remark or observation…and yet God in His sovereignty drops it like a seed into ready and tender soil. And, somehow, it takes root. Weeks, months, years, maybe even generations later, one of the children will say, "I remember the day when…."

How do these wondrous encounters happen?

I can tell you this, it won't happen while you're sitting around the tube watching *The Simpsons*. With all my heart, I believe it is the forethought and creativity of caring parents who open the door for such divine transactions to penetrate young souls and change life and perceptions forever.

In my book, at least, that is no small thing.

A Compassionate

CHAPTER FOUR

Love

Thomas Kinkade

 lothe yourselves with tenderhearted mercy, kindness, humility, gentleness, and patience.

COLOSSIANS 3:12, NLT

EVEN AN APOSTLE BECOMES WEARY NOW AND THEN.

The Twelve had gathered around Jesus following their first mission trip, and it was probably one of those times when everyone in that little band was thinking the exact same thing: *We want to kick back a little, grab a bite to eat, put our feet up, and have a few hours of debriefing time with the Lord.*

Jesus wanted that, too. Trouble was, Scripture tells us, "so many people were coming and going that they did not even have a chance to eat."

His heart went out to those who so desperately needed guidance and attention and words of life.

"Come with me by yourselves," Jesus said, "to a quiet place and get some rest."

It was a good plan, but it wasn't to be. When the people saw Jesus and the disciples get into a boat to escape to a solitary place, they "ran on foot from all the towns and got there ahead of them."

So much for the mini-retreat and rest time! When the disciples stepped out of the boat to see the pressing, reaching, noisy throng, who would have blamed them for feeling a little angry or disgusted?

Jesus saw the crowd, too, but instead of being upset or impatient with them, "he had compassion on them, because they were like sheep without a shepherd. So he began teaching them many things" (see Mark 6:34).

The teaching went on until late in the day, drawing toward evening.

You might have expected that.

Because you can't do compassion in a hurry.

Compassion takes time.

It wasn't convenient. It wasn't His first choice. It wasn't according to plan. But His heart went out to those who so desperately needed guidance and attention and words of life. And Jesus took the time. He acknowledged their struggles and disappointments and He determined to give of Himself to meet their needs.

What a perfect model for parents in a distracted, often selfish, overly busy world. It's a reminder to sometimes-preoccupied dads and moms to be sensitive to those sighs, frowns, slumped shoulders, occasional tears, and disparaging, defeatist comments. It's so easy to brush right past them in our busyness. It's so easy to rationalize our failure to meet needs under our own roof.

Jesus, however, saw the crowds and took compassion on them. In the same way, parents need to take compassion on discouraged children—whether they are four or twenty-four.

And no matter what anyone tells you, you can't do that on the run.

It will take a sacrificial investment of time.

Nanette: 🌿

$\mathcal{I}$f this book is an honest peek behind the curtains of the Kinkade home, then you have to know that slowing down enough to show compassion to our children is one of our highest priorities.

It's also a never-ending challenge.

As with many others, our lives could easily become so busy, so complicated, and so overcommitted that our children might begin to feel "lower priority" to Thom and me—and even to themselves. *And we simply can't allow that to happen.*

You may have experienced similar pressures. Sometimes

when we're trying to get out the door for some meeting or function, our whole focus becomes "getting there on time." Thom or I might find ourselves raising our voices to the level of a Marine Corps drill sergeant (you feel like you just have to, sometimes, if only to be *heard*), barking out the command, "Everybody in the car, *now!*"

Let's face it, in those moments, we're not in tune with the feelings, concerns, and fears of each of our children. Consumed by our goal of "getting somewhere," we disregard the moment, and close our eyes to immediate needs. If that sort of lifestyle continues, if we allow it to become habitual, we can become hardened to the emotions and concerns of our children—things that don't seem very significant to our adult minds, but may be *very* important to them.

How we need the grace of God to use that simple word *no* more often! Really in every facet of our lives...in business, in hobbies, in kids' activities and sports, even in church obligations. How quickly and easily we tend to pile activity upon activity, event upon event, commitment upon commitment. In the midst of such frenzy, you could end up becoming so harried and distracted that you rarely find a place of peace, a place where you sense the Holy Spirit working through you to nurture and encourage troubled hearts.

As much as we may wish it otherwise, we simply cannot express compassionate love when we are running full tilt from morning until night. It is almost impossible to offer compassion in a hurry.

Compassionate parenting is *living in* your kids' lives—just as I allow Nanette to live in my life, and she allows me in hers. My wife and I include each other in our daily struggles and triumphs. The good and the bad. The decision-making and the frustrations. Every part of us comes to the forefront as we spend our evenings together.

On an admittedly different level, we try to do this with our kids, too. We include ourselves in their lives. If they've experienced something exciting or encouraging (or funny!), we ask them to tell us about it, to relive it for us. In our first book, *The Many Loves of Marriage*, I spoke about the fact that I really don't feel as though I've lived through something until I've had the opportunity to share it with Nanette. Our girls, I think, feel somewhat the same way about sharing with the family. They have come to the place where they just assume that their experiences are family experiences. They expect to share them. They know there will be time and opportunity. They anticipate that we will listen and give them our full attention.

Not long ago, Merritt took a weeklong eighth grade class trip to Washington, D.C. She'd looked forward to this trip all year, and yet after she was there for only a few days, she suffered an attack of homesickness. Our reaction, as we spoke to her on the phone, was to just let her express it, offering sympathy and encouragement as we were able.

When she came home, we made her the star of the show! We really put her up on a pedestal for the way she represented the Kinkade family and asked her to speak to the family and share her memories of everything she had done and seen. She had kept a journal, and we asked her to read all of the entries to us, so we could join in those experiences with her.

What fun we had cheering her on, and it seemed to mean so much to her that we made her first trip without the family the centerpiece of a family gathering and celebration.

When you stop to think about it, what's more compassionate than truly *listening* to someone with all your interest and all your

What's more compassionate than truly listening to someone with all your interest and all your heart?

heart? What's more encouraging than realizing that someone you care about really desires to enter your life...to get swept up in your excitement...to shoulder your disappointment and hurt...to listen to your crazy ideas and laugh at your dumb jokes? I believe that being *truly heard* is one of the most fulfilling experiences in all of life. A true listener shows compassionate love without even lifting a finger.

> *I believe that being truly heard is one of the most fulfilling experiences in all of life.*

Compassion is living within the skin of another person, if only temporarily. Walking a mile in their proverbial moccasins. It involves responding to their weaknesses with a little extra understanding, rather than simply "reacting" to those words and actions that so irritate you or try your patience.

One of our daughters is at a very challenging phase in her life. As a result, she's been very demanding—almost insisting on that spotlight of focused attention. Nanette, living with this attitude for many more hours than I do each day, has felt a little beat up by these highly emotional verbal demands. As we've discussed the situation, she's shared with me that our daughter is just "too uptight, too demanding, too worked up over every little thing." As you might expect, any parent's natural tendency would be to get a little fed up with it all, to begin pushing back a little and saying, "I don't have to put up with this."

As difficult as it might be right now, I've tried to encourage Nanette to just step into our daughter's skin for a little bit, trying to understand what might be behind the insecurity and hyper-sensitivity. Is it some fear she can't express? Is it hormones? What's going on here? When only one wheel out of four seems to be squeaking *loudly*, that's the one that needs the extra oil, the extra attention. "Let's just give her as much focus and love as we can right now," I suggested. "Maybe we ought to let her get away with a little bit more than what we allow with the other kids because she's at such a needy phase of her life right now."

It's compassionate to recognize and deal with the *reality* of your child's life and situation—not some mythical ideal or vaunted expectation that you've read in a book or formed in your head over the years. Being a good parent means realistically assessing your children and their situations day by day and year by year. You may not even understand their struggles, their fears, or their anger, but you can be there when they need you and step into their lives to the best of your ability.

Once again, however, you can't pull it off in fifteen minutes of "quality time" each day. And the busier you become with commitments outside the home, the less chance you will have of pulling it off at all.

One such painful near miss in my life comes to mind very clearly.

A NEAR MISS

For Chandler, who has loved school since she could scramble up into a little wooden school chair and focus her eyes on a blackboard, it was a most special, exciting night.

I can't imagine open house night at school being that much of a big deal for our other girls. But for Chandler, it was *huge*. Looking back, I really think I had the best of intentions when I brought along a business associate to the function. After all, he was thinking of sending his children to the same Christian school. So it just made sense to invite him, right? And, well, there was no denying his importance to our future business. What could it harm? I could accomplish two things at once: affirm my daughter and develop a relationship with a valuable business contact—no small feat in this demanding, fast-paced world.

So there was Chandler on one side of me, my daughter who needed every bit of extra attention and affirmation right now, pulling on my sleeve and saying, "Dad, I want to show you my sixth grade class!"

Meanwhile, on my other side, there was this gentleman I had invited, politely awaiting a tour of the facilities.

I remember thinking something like this: *There are several good reasons for showing this guy around tonight. It would be really great for this little Christian school if his son came on board. Who knows where that would lead? Besides, I want to minister to him. I want to bless him. And I can't deny that it would be good for the business if I could get him plugged into this community. I'd better take him over to the kindergarten and introduce him to the teacher.*

Chandler pulled on my arm. "C'mon, Dad! Lemme show you my stuff!"

"Just a minute, okay, Chandler? I *do* want to come over and see your class and your work, but I've got to help this man get over to the kindergarten area first."

"Okay," she said. But I couldn't help noticing the quick flash of disappointment in her eyes.

I took my guest to the kindergarten room, showed him around, and introduced him to the headmaster. The three of us had (what I thought was) the briefest of conversations. In all honesty, I lost track of time for a few minutes. In my absence, Chandler began showing Nanette all her art projects and essays, and my wife was at her affirming, encouraging best.

After a few more minutes, I finally excused myself from the conversation. "You guys go ahead and talk." I smiled as I backed out of the room.

Hurrying over to my daughter's classroom, I found Nanette... but no Chandler.

"Where's Chandler?" I asked.

"Oh, she's gone."

"Gone?"

"Out to play. She showed us everything."

"But wait a minute!" I protested. "I didn't get to see anything."

Nanette could have said, "Well, *where were you?*" But she didn't reply. It was one of those classic, sinking moments when reality suddenly impacts your skull with the force of an errant shot put.

Kinkade, you are such an idiot! Just look at what you've done! You just clearly announced to Chandler that Dad doesn't really care about the most important thing in her life right now—her schoolwork.

I felt sick inside. *What could I do now?*

> *Moments of parenting are too quick and fleeting to piggyback with other priorities.*

That's the way it is, sometimes, isn't it? The moments of life keep coming at you, like water from a fire hose, and you have to make decisions about what to do with them. You don't have to be a Rhodes scholar to realize there are opportunities with your children that will never be repeated.

The moment is there, and then it is gone.

Yes, certainly, there will be other moments, other opportunities. But not *that* one.

I immediately tried to repair the damage. I remember striding across the graveled playground in the warm California twilight, calling her name. I finally found her with a group of friends.

"Chandler!" I called out as I walked toward her. "Chandler, I'm sorry I missed you! I wanted to see your art. I wanted to look at your assignments."

"Oh," she said, "they're in there. They're sitting on my desk." She started to turn away.

"No, honey, I want you to *show* me. I want to hear the story behind each one."

We went back into the classroom, and there was never a more engaged, attentive father than Thomas Kinkade in that moment. We did end up having a meaningful time, and if she was still a little offended it certainly didn't show.

But it reinforced a lesson in my heart. The moments of parenting are too quick and fleeting to piggyback with other priorities. And if we are overly absorbed in ten thousand activities and pastimes outside the home, we're simply not going to be there to maximize those opportunities. Life will go on (as it tends to do), *but it won't be the life it might have been.* We will lose track of our children's needs, and our attempts at compassion will fall short of the mark.

God helping me, I'm not going to let that happen.

*Then little children
were brought to Jesus
for him to place
his hands on them
and pray for them.*

MATTHEW 19:13

A Family-Centered

CHAPTER FIVE

Love

I am still not all I should be, but I am focusing all my energies on this one thing: Forgetting the past and looking forward to what lies ahead.

PHILIPPIANS 3:13, NLT

WHEN I WAS GROWING UP IN PLACERVILLE, THERE WAS ONE HOME I ADMIRED ABOVE ALL OTHERS.

The dad in the family happened to be my youth pastor, Mac DeWater.

I remember being captivated by this family's creativity. They never had much money (I could certainly identify with that), and they didn't have many opportunities to go places or see the wide world beyond the borders of our little town, but I will tell you what they *did* have.

They always had a lot of fun.

They just seemed to like being with each other and doing things together. The rooms of that home were filled with animated conversation and laughter, and it drew me like a moth to a porch light.

In our town, the high school junior-senior prom was one of *the* big events of the social calendar. To hear some of the kids talk, however, it seemed like many anticipated the unofficial party *after* the prom even more than the main event. At that second gathering, usually held in some nearby park after

> *The rooms of that home were filled with animated conversation and laughter, and it drew me like a moth to a porch light.*

the formal school function wound down, there was a big bon-
fire, plenty of beer, passionate embraces in the shadows beyond
the firelight, and occasional drunken fistfights among the guys.

Remember, this was the permissive seventies—the decade
following the turmoil and "new tolerance" of the sixties. I really
can't imagine a scenario like this in Placerville these days.

I've no doubt that back then, however, several of the local pas-
tors railed against those activities—and rightly so. But Mac
had a bit different approach.

He decided to throw an after-prom party of his own.

The DeWaters opened the doors of their home for couples
who wanted somewhere safe to come hang out for a while
after the big dance. And this was where the family creativity
kicked in. They all pitched in to decorate their large basement
and turn it into a replica of an old-fashioned fifties soda foun-
tain. They set up their stereo downstairs, put a stack of oldies
on the turntable, and had a "sock hop"—along with several
other crazy games and activities (and plenty of munchies).

You might think this sounded rather bland and tame com-
pared to the "passion in the park" party. But the truth is, it
really caught on. In fact, for several years running, it became *the*
party in town—the very center of social life after the prom.
Virtually everyone wanted to come to that party instead of
the wild one. In fact, it became so crowded and popular that
someone literally had to direct traffic outside the pastor's home.

There were no parking places within a mile of that block, and it was standing room only in the house from top to bottom.

The truth was, most of the kids really didn't want to do the gross stuff...*all they needed was a viable alternative.* Somewhere to go. Somewhere to be. Somewhere to be seen in all their finery. A little bit of fun and a few more laughs before the gown went back in the closet, the tux went back to the rental shop, and the Big Night was history.

I'm just radical enough to believe that the very same dynamic can hold true in a family.

STRONGER THAN PEER GROUPS

A few pages back, Nanette and I mentioned some of the changes we noticed in Merritt's life after she began attending a different school and spending time with a new group of friends.

There's nothing surprising in that.

In fact, whenever you see something surprising in your child's behavior, chances are better than average that you can begin with his or her peer orientation. That's where moms and dads get a big clue that they need to be more proactive in creating a fun, engaging family environment—to counterbalance the outside pressures.

One of the great fallacies of the pop psychology that has infiltrated our culture is the notion that some mysterious, powerful force called "The Peer Group" is just waiting to unleash its irresistible magnetic force on your child the moment he or she turns thirteen. We're led to believe that this will be hands down the most influential, formational force in your child's life and that a mother or father has little hope of counteracting its effects.

On one level, that view does have some validity. Because if you don't take family experience and home experience to a level of interactivity, fun, and identity, then, yes, you have good reason to fear the peer group. If all your kids are getting at home is the drone of the television and a bunch of bored, preoccupied family members lounging around, then there certainly will be a strong vacuum in their hearts. They will turn to the peer group because that's the only affirmation they can find.

Family interaction and fun doesn't have much to do with money.

But is it inevitable?

I don't believe it for a minute. *It doesn't have to happen that way.* It's really a matter of paying attention to several of the things we've already touched on in this little book: vigilance, focus, creativity, and compassion.

Let me emphasize again that family interaction and fun doesn't have much to do with money. (Pastor Mac and his wife barely had enough to keep the bills paid.) But it has a great deal to do with where the priorities of your heart truly lie. If you set your heart to treat your spouse and your children as your hobby, your favorite pastime—even your obsession—you will begin to discover a force that matches and exceeds the drawing power

of any peer group on the planet.

It is the drawing power of an active, happy family.

Think, for instance, of the time you would spend if you decided to take up golf. If you wanted to really accomplish anything out on the links, you would need to watch a few videos, browse your local golf shop, read some magazine articles on technique, do some workouts at the putting green and driving range, and maybe even get a little private instruction from a pro at the golf course. As I've told several of my friends, if you took even half that level of effort and interest and applied it to finding new ways of keeping your family active and well integrated, you would reap phenomenal results.

To be candid, there aren't very many engaged families around these days. Most families are just in neutral.

Sometimes I'll hear someone say, "We really had some quality family time last night."

That always piques my interest, so I'll say, "Really? What did you do?"

"Oh, we popped a big bag of popcorn and watched a couple videos together."

There's nothing wrong with that, but in my book it does *not* qualify as "quality family time." When you think about it, that's just putting in passive, neutral hours together. What

I'm talking about is getting out of neutral and getting into *drive* as a family. Going somewhere. Interacting with each other. Meshing the gears of personalities. Doing something together. Talking. Playing. Competing. Sharing. Exploring. Learning. Creating some memories that will shine in the mind's eye for years and years beyond the vague recollections of one more forgettable movie.

You are the parent...*you* be the driver. *You* keep them on track. *You* keep them focused. *You* keep them plugged into family activities. *You* keep them pointed in a healthy direction. Give yourself to the effort. Sacrifice for it. Pray for massive infusions of God's strength and wisdom. Reach for it every day.

Or...simply yield to the flow of contemporary culture. And don't be taken aback when your children follow right along where that current is leading.

It's really very simple. If you view motherhood and fatherhood as a passive thing—that your job basically consists of providing them with food, clothing, and shelter until they're old enough to survive on their own—then you may be raising your children, but you are not parenting them.

Parenting means daily involvement. It means fighting the battle for the hearts and minds and futures of the boys and girls, the young men and women, God has placed in your charge.

Here's a simple example. Let's imagine your preteen son says to you, "Hey Mom, hey Dad, a lot of kids I know are getting into skateboarding. I want to get into that, too. Can I get a skateboard?"

Well, skateboarding may be okay. But maybe in your town it's not okay. Maybe the skateboarders in your town are a particular subculture with a particular outlook that flies in the face of your family values. Nanette and I might respond to that sort of situation like this: "That's cool that the kids in your school are getting into skateboarding. I can see how that might be fun. But do you know what? We're the Kinkades, and our family does things the Kinkade way. Our family likes to go horseback riding (or hiking or sledding or fishing or sailboating or four-wheeling or whatever). So why don't you invite some of your friends to go with us on our next family adventure, and we'll really have some fun."

> *Parenting means fighting the battle for the hearts and minds and futures of the boys and girls, the young men and women, God has placed in your charge.*

Skateboarding and the subculture loses much of its drawing power when there is a strong, engaging activity available as an alternative. We've done that in so many instances in our family. Instead of just rolling over and surrendering to the current preoccupations of our culture, we proactively pursue our own adventures and fun activities.

PUT OFF, PUT ON

Nanette and I call this response our "put off, put on" principle. In Scripture, Paul talks about "putting off" the old mindset, the old habits, the old ways of doing things, and "putting on" the new attitudes and character traits of a man or woman in Christ. You don't just junk your old set of clothes; you step into a fresh, new set of clothes provided by the Lord. In a similar way, we wouldn't tell our girls, "We don't want you hanging out at the mall all weekend with the kids." We would say, "Why don't we take up the hobby of playing tennis as a family?" And that's just what we did recently. We're not very good...but we are together.

Substitute something that could potentially be out of your control as a parent with something that will remain within your control. It makes no sense to simply forbid activities or associations—and then provide nothing in its place!

Though it may not seem like it right now, the years you have with your children will race by faster than you think.

But that would take so much work! you may be thinking. *That would take so much forethought and planning and investment of time and resources.*

That's true. It does and it will. Following this plan could mean rearranging your life, and Nanette and I can't make that decision for you. It isn't easy for us, either. I'm a full time artist with a large enterprise on my hands, and Nanette is a busy homemaker with four children, who is also involved in decisions related to the business.

A family-centered love is a juggling act because you're also trying to lead a life as an adult, with a multitude of adult responsibilities and relationships. But having said that, everyone has some hours they control. (If you don't, then you're too busy anyway!) And how will you invest those hours? What will you do with that time after you've jumped through all the necessary hoops in the adult world? Many people will say, "I need to zone out. I just need time for me." They'll tell you that they're simply too tired or too burned out to invest themselves in meaningful experiences with their families. (So why did they even choose to *have* a family?)

My modest proposal in answer to that is: Go ahead and find some activities that you enjoy and that renew your spirit, *but take the kids along for the ride, too.* Let them participate. Be with them. Be together.

Though it may not seem like it right now, the years you have with your children will race by faster than you think. It won't be but a few years until you have that "time alone" again. You'll have all the peace and quiet you can handle. You'll have opportunity to do many of those things you've been desiring to do. But if you have invested your life in your children through their growing-up years at home, if you have poured yourself into the life and health of your family, the difference will be this: You'll be satisfied. You'll be at peace. You won't find yourself plagued with feelings of guilt or gnawing regret. You'll know in your heart that you made the most of those years with your children God gave you.

You'll have the memories.

You'll have the photographs.

You'll have the crazy souvenirs and mementos.

It takes thought. It takes planning. It takes prayer, and as Nanette has said, the help of Almighty God Himself.

There are no guarantees, but chances are very good that you'll also have that deep-down joy of looking at adult children who are well adjusted and strongly committed to the Lord and to your family values.

I've never heard of anyone reaching their retirement years and saying, "My greatest regret in life is that I spent too much time with my family. Oh, if only I hadn't invested all that time in my spouse and my children!" You can go from house to house in a retirement community or assisted living center, and you will never hear anyone say that.

But you may very well hear someone say, "My only regret is that I wasn't there for my kids. I just didn't make family a priority. I was too busy chasing a career, chasing dollars, building a business (or even being consumed by ministry), and the years were gone before I knew it."

We can't do anything about the past, but the wonderful thing about life—wherever we may be—is that we can challenge ourselves right now to do better. If we still have kids at home, we can ask ourselves, "How can I refocus my life to create time with my family, to create opportunities with my kids, to create chances to build memories? How can I strategically make the most of these few years before they slip away from me?"

Every year should have weeklong family bonding times.

Every month should have daylong family bonding times.

Every day should have hour-long (or even ten-minute-long) family bonding times.

It takes thought. It takes planning. It takes prayer, and as Nanette has said, the help of Almighty God Himself. But unlike so many other investments and activities, no one will say at the end of it all, "It just wasn't worth it."

As I reflect on my growing-up years in Placerville, I don't think I can remember one point from any of the lessons or sermons I heard from the youth pastor.

But I will never forget the laughter in the walls of his home.

He showed a boy from a broken home what it means to love your family, and it's one of the richest gifts I think I will ever receive.

A Visionary

CHAPTER SIX

Love, Part 1

How precious are your thoughts about me, O God!
They are innumerable!
I can't even count them;
they outnumber the grains of sand!

PSALM 139:17–18, NLT

GOD HAS A VISION FOR EACH OF HIS
CHILDREN—EVEN WHEN WE'VE LOST
THE VISION FOR OURSELVES.

Both of us
were inspired
to dream
about what
we might become.

lert, compassionate parents can help

their children through discouraging times

by keeping a vision before their eyes...an

assurance that they will be used mightily by

the Lord as they obey Him, love Him, and

serve Him, enabling them to become what

they never dreamed they could become and

do what they never imagined they could do.

Both Thom and I were blessed as children

with positive examples of individuals who

served God with their lives and also excelled

in their chosen professions. Both of us were

inspired to dream about what we might

become. For Thom, it was an artist; for me, it

was a nurse and a homemaker. We had parents who truly believed in us and encouraged us to pursue our dreams.

As I seek to do that with our children, I think of Jeremiah 29:11: "'For I know the plans I have for you,' declares the LORD, 'plans to prosper you and not to harm you, plans to give you hope and a future.'"

That's God's Word for our children. They need to know that truth, and as parents we need to remember it. *He has a plan for each of His children. He has a plan for each of our children.* And they are extraordinary plans, conceived in the mind of God Himself.

Early on in the parenting process, I can remember feeling a little paralyzed sometimes, fearful of making some major mistake or misstep that would damage my child for life. *What if I say the wrong thing at the wrong time? What if I go here and do this when I should have gone there and done that? This is the biggest job of my life! What if I botch it up?*

Since that time, I've come to rest more in the sovereign

care of God. He knows I want the best for my girls, and His protective, guiding hand is upon each one of them. Thomas and I will certainly make mistakes as fallible, human parents, yet God Himself continues His shaping, refining work in the lives of Evie, Winsor, Chandler, and Merritt as we pray for them and entrust them to His divine care.

As much as we might wish it, they may not have a smooth path in life. In fact, most likely there will be great heartache and trials along the way. But God promises to use all things and work all things together for good in our lives so that with every passing day we might be more like His Son (see Romans 8:28–29).

In Thom's life, God even used his mother and father's divorce. Though it was tragic and sad, God worked through those events. It was a hard and painful thing for a boy to endure, but the experience and the sorrow were not wasted (as he will describe in a few pages).

Our girls are growing up with a mother and father who

love them and love each other, but I'm sure there are difficulties and struggles in their lives that I'm not even aware of—and may never fully understand. Even so, I believe that God will use those things to strengthen their character and teach them the all-important lesson of dependence on Him.

Through all my years at home, my parents faithfully encouraged me in my gifts and abilities, opening my eyes to how I might begin using them. We're trying to do the same with our children, too.

As parents, our role is to simply make such opportunities available, pouring on the affirmation!

Merritt, we believe, has a real gift for teaching. With a little encouragement and logistical support from Thom and me, she has developed her own swim instruction school. It's been a delight to see this unfold. Her patience and her ability to instruct these children has just amazed us. She has actually developed her own little business—organized the whole thing and taken all the courses she needs to be certified and qualified. She's put together a schedule, done all the calling, and really followed through.

We're trying to let her discover those gifts—and then just flourish in them. She's also teaching in Sunday school, presenting lessons every week, and being with the children and nurturing them.

As parents, our role is to simply make such opportunities available, pouring on the affirmation! We want to give each of our girls the self-esteem to recognize that they can attempt worthy goals and succeed—or learn valuable lessons in the attempting! We want them to feel good about who God created them to be.

Nanette: THE GOD HUNT

The youth culture of the twenty-first century has been so tainted by the negativism and nihilism of our day that parents have a real job on their hands trying to keep a positive vision of the future before their children's eyes.

As we've already mentioned, Thomas and I believe in filtering out as much of that dark, toxic material from our home as we possibly can. Eliminating TV was a huge step in that direction. The music in our home is Christian music, with life-building lyrics. We believe in curbing as much negative, hateful, sensual input as we can, recognizing that there is plenty of negativism out there to spare and that our children will be exposed to it sooner or later anyway—hopefully *later*, and in smaller doses.

Then, with God's help, we continually point out the positive things we've seen and experienced throughout the day, focusing on those things, and giving God the glory for what He has done. That certainly seems to be the spirit of Paul's words in 1 Thessalonians:

Be joyful always; pray continually; give thanks in all circumstances, for this is God's will for you in Christ Jesus. (5:16–18)

We have a little activity we like to do in our family that we call "the God hunt." Throughout our day, we look for the hand of God—His touch—in our life situations or in any blessing that comes our way. It could be as simple as finding a parking place on a busy afternoon or as great as having a dear friend healed from an illness. We walk through the sunlight hours keeping our eyes focused on Him, watching for His fingerprints and footprints all around us. It's surprising to all of us what a difference that makes in our day. And I think that is a very powerful antidote to the poisons of the negative society we live in.

When you start focusing on God, you find Him everywhere!

Besides that, it's just so much fun! The more you look, the more you see. When you start focusing on God, you find Him everywhere! You see Him in so many details of your life. You begin to understand how infinitely He cares about us—and even the minutia of our days.

I love the words of David on this theme:

How precious are your thoughts about me, O God!

They are innumerable!

I can't even count them;

> they outnumber the grains of sand!

And when I wake up in the morning

> you are still with me!

(PSALM 139:17–18, NLT)

As these concepts take root in the minds of children, they gain a growing sense of security and peace. They are empowered to recognize that, *My heavenly Father is in control of this whole world—and He loves me! Maybe things aren't as bad as they seem sometimes.*

As they gradually yield their lives and their dreams to the Lord, our children can be assured that they have a God who is ultimately looking out for them and working for their good. When you think about it, how can you lose?

Thom and I have discussed these things many times. We've come to the conclusion that throughout the lives of our children, our constant objective is to transfer them from our parenting to the parenting of God the

Father—to help them and encourage them to relate to Him as early and often as possible. Our end goal as parents is to enable and urge our children to have a personal relationship—that wonderful, transforming friendship—with the living God. If that is *all* we do as parents, then we have succeeded. If our kids have Christ, they have it all.

He will always be there for them. He will never fail them nor forsake them—even after Thom and I have left this earth.

> *Our end goal as parents is to enable and urge our children to have a personal relationship with the living God.*

What a comfort that is to me as a mother. Although my girls have been given to me to love and nurture, it is the Lord who created them in the womb and brought them into the world and is developing them for His good and for His purposes. In the truest sense of the word, the Kinkade girls are only on loan to Thom and me. They are the Lord's.

All of our children are uniquely created by Him and will be uniquely used by Him. We tell them that over and over, praying that the truth will grip them as it has gripped their dad and mom.

When you think of the "many loves of parenting," you will realize that He *is* the parent with many loves.

In fact, it's a love that will never end. ❧

A parent's carefully selected, prayerfully prepared words can have a mighty effect as they intersect with the lives of vulnerable, growing children. This is particularly true in what I call "vision casting"—using compelling words to describe a possible future for a child.

Who can calculate the impact of timely spoken words?

Solomon said: "Like apples of gold in settings of silver, so is a word spoken at the right moment" (Proverbs 25:11, MLB). The right word at the right time shines like exquisitely crafted jewelry—and is even more precious.

James speaks to the sheer power of words, reminding us that the tongue is like a rudder on a great ship. It can take that massive craft into safe harbor, or it can drive it onto the rocks.

You may not be able to perform a ballet in front of your kids to show them what it's like to be a dancer, but you might be able to speak with passion about how wonderful it is to see the art of movement in a body. You might be able to paint a picture with your words about the privilege of blessing and inspiring people as a ballet dancer—or a musician, or a writer, or a teacher, or a devoted homemaker.

As parents, we should never take this potential for granted. As God opens the door, we have the opportunity to sketch out compelling ideas and thoughts that prompt young hearts to begin thinking about their possibilities, their potential, and their future.

This may sound a little strange, but how long has it been since you've asked your child, "What do you want to be when you grow up?"

Initially, that may sound like one of the most inane, off-the-shelf questions an adult could ask of a child. Everyone says that to a stranger's kid, mostly just to make conversation.

But if *you* ask it of your child, you will not be "just making conversation." You will be the right person asking the right question at the right time. You'll be probing one of the most troubling, exciting, motivating areas of your child's heart: his or her future.

Have you asked it of your children lately?

I asked it of Chandler, just a few nights ago. *"What do you want to be when you grow up, Chandler?"*

She looked at me, knew that I was serious, and pondered her reply for a moment. "You know, Dad, I've been thinking

about that. I really have a heart for homeless people. For some reason, I'd like to be able to run, like, umm…a hotel for homeless people."

Now that one caught me by surprise. I was fascinated by what was going on in her heart that would lead her to such a desire. Was this something the Lord had planted and had been nurturing for some time unbeknownst to Nanette and me?

Ultimately, the vision that matters most for my child is God's vision.

"Well," I replied, "you know about all the work we do with charities. Maybe someday we could come up with money out of our family charity to actually do that—to get a building somewhere. Maybe you could work there and help people like that."

"I think if they had a place to stay, maybe they could change their life."

"You could be right, Chandler. You know how much I love homeless people and try to help them. Hey—did you ever notice that old Victorian house down the street from our house? The one with the big porch?"

She nodded.

"You know, that's where a lot of older people and mentally disabled people live, and the staff there works with them."

"I know, Dad. And I've been wanting to go down there." (Another surprise to me.)

"Have you, Chandler? Well, maybe when you get just a little bit older, we can go there together, and we'll meet the people who run it. Maybe you could get a job there someday, helping people."

Suddenly Chandler was excited. "Oh! I'd *love* that, Dad!"

Do you see how that conversation got started? It began with *Chandler's* dreams, not mine. It started with what the Lord might be working in her heart, rather than in my heart. But with just a little bit of interest and interaction, I had the opportunity to cast a vision before her eyes—a vision of how she could begin to help people and make a difference. It was an exciting moment for both of us.

Ultimately, the vision that matters most for my child isn't my vision or Nanette's vision or their grandparents' vision; it is *God's* vision.

Yes, we certainly seek to represent God to our children when they are small, and we have the responsibility to train, nurture, and model righteous living to our kids. But there is definitely a point in a child's life at which our role diminishes, and God's role in their life in a one-on-one relationship begins to gain traction.

We are not the vision-setters for our children—as much as we would like to think so in our human pride. It's always sad when you see a parent attempting to live vicariously through the life of his or her child. Yet it happens all too often. A dad, for instance, may attempt to atone for his own foolishness, lack of vision, or missed opportunities by forcing his young son down a certain path toward a certain end. Maybe he'd always wanted to be a football player—and by golly, his son won't miss that chance like he did! Never mind that the boy has no inclination or desire in that direction and hates competition!

Is college a right choice for every young person? Not necessarily! In fact, God may have other plans. Yet the knee-jerk reaction of so many parents would be to say, "*Of course* you're going to college! You *have* to go to college if you want to get ahead in life!"

> *Visionary parents are those who cling to a vision of God's guiding hand in their children's lives....*

Nanette and I have thought about that. What if one of our daughters said to us, "Dad, Mom, I really don't want to go to college. I know in my heart that I'm called to be a wife and mother." In my pride, I would be inclined to argue with her—to convince her that a college degree is the only way to go.

But how could I be certain that I wasn't interfering with God's plan and desire for her at that point? Out of love for her and trust in God, I hope I could reply, "Wherever God leads you, honey. Just be sure to walk with Him."

A visionary parent is not a parent who says, "I have a vision for my child's life and future." Visionary parents are those who cling to a vision of God's guiding hand in their children's lives...parents who inspire their sons and daughters to believe in the potential of their lives, but refuse to dictate that potential.

Parenting is a grave responsibility all wrapped up in a delightful opportunity. To stand by your own children, to walk with them, to help them understand God's place for them in our troubled, needy world, and to persuade them that in their own faith they can be used by God to change that world is a wonder beyond my reckoning.

Vision! Don't miss the priceless opportunity to enter into your child's thoughts and questions and longings about the future.

Think it through with them.

Talk it out.

And don't be afraid to dream a little.

A Visionary

CHAPTER SEVEN

Love, Part 2

Thomas Kinkade

 And you yourself must be an example to them.

TITUS 2:7, NLT

AS I WAS GROWING UP, MOST OF MY
FRIENDS HAD REAL FATHERS AT HOME.

Dads who went to work in the morning, came
home at night, did handyman jobs around the
house on Saturday, went to their sons' ball games,
and provided a sense of stability and security in
their families. I longed for such a father—a dad
who would be there for me, care about me, and do
things with me. As it turned out, that wasn't what
God provided in my life.

But in His kindness and grace, He did something
else for me.

He provided me with three surrogate fathers who
deeply inspired me, built into my life, and shaped
my future by their teaching, example, and friendship. Their visionary love gave a fatherless teenager
a reason to hope in the future, a reason to dream.

The first was a man I've written about several
times: my youth pastor, Mac DeWater. In fact,
he's still a close friend to this day. Mac was the one
who set a model and vision of family life before

Their visionary love gave a fatherless teenager a reason to hope in the future, a reason to dream.

my eyes, opening up a pathway I've walked ever since. He was a pastor, a rancher, and a dad with five kids who seemed to be involved in everything but was never too busy to offer a word of encouragement—or even pull me and several of his own kids along on one of his ventures.

From Mac, I learned that dads can be a lot of fun—and don't have to take themselves too seriously. He would always be promoting wild contests and stunts, and somehow the DeWaters never ran out of fun things to do as a family. He touched my life at a young age and cast a vision of home as a place of laughter, love, creativity, and togetherness, even in the face of difficulties and trials. In the midst of it all, I caught glimpses of Mac's Lord, Jesus Christ.

I wanted to be like both of them.

THE DISCIPLINE OF FINISHING

My second surrogate dad was Charlie Bell, owner of the local sign shop where I began working at age twelve. What a divine appointment that was! Charlie was a consummate craftsman and probably the most fascinating man I'd ever met. In the eyes of a twelve-year-old boy, he'd been everywhere and done everything. His stories fired my imagination with scenes of exotic, faraway places and adventures that set my heart yearning for the world beyond Placerville.

Charlie had carefully ordered his life in a way beyond anything I'd ever experienced or even imagined. He built his own house by hand. He customized his own car. He designed and built boats and wrote articles for shipbuilding magazines. He was an excellent watercolor painter and a master of sign techniques and every kind of lettering. In previous years, he'd been an amateur entertainer and a circus clown.

When I began to work for him, he was a lean, trim seventy-year-old, and as far as I was concerned, there wasn't anything Charlie Bell couldn't do. Most wondrous of all, he took a young boy with energy, ambition, and desire right under his wing and became my mentor, teacher, and friend.

One of the most life-shaping lessons I learned from Charlie Bell was the discipline of *finishing* a job. "Thom," he would tell me, "don't you even start a job unless you know you can finish it. And once you do start, then you *have* to finish it." For Charlie, this was the law of the Medes and the Persians—an integral part of his whole moral code.

It was also something new to me. As a kid, I'd always started all kinds of odd jobs, paintings, and art projects, but once I got them to a certain point, I would lose interest or get discouraged and abandon them.

Not after I began working with Charlie!

From then on, and to this day, I finish *everything*. I pride myself on my ability to overcome any puzzle or problem on any painting and keep moving ahead. Throughout my career, I have never started a painting and not finished it.

(Although there are some I've had around the studio for a few years and then gotten back to them and finished them later.) Perhaps you've heard of young artists who start a painting and then say, "I've got to throw this away. It's no good anymore. It's all wrong and there's nothing I can do with it."

Because of the legacy of Charlie Bell, I have never said that. The truth is, you *can* do something with most any project that comes to mind: You can finish it. I've had a painting with an eight-inch hole right in the middle of the canvas and still been able to repair it, restore it, and complete the work.

The formula I learned from Charlie is very simple: Effort plus passion equals completion. If you put in the hours—the raw, rote hours—and maintain a passion for the task, you can complete virtually anything you start.

> *The formula I learned from Charlie is very simple: Effort plus passion equals completion.*

Charlie built his business and his life around tireless effort, grit and determination, and iron discipline. He taught and modeled those skills to me with patience and kindness, and gave me a hunger and desire to accomplish something with my life.

THE HIGH CALLING

My third surrogate dad was Glen Wessels.

I remember the day at age fourteen when I walked out into our yard in Placerville and noticed some builders working on an abandoned barn in the field next to our house. What in the world could they be up to with that old place? Curious, I walked the hundred yards or so over to the barn and asked the workmen what they were doing.

One of them paused before swinging his hammer. "We're renovating this barn for an artist who's moving into town. He's gonna turn it into an art studio."

I was thunderstruck by those words. I could hardly believe my ears.

"*What?*" I said. "Did you say an *art studio?*"

It seemed completely miraculous to me. A bolt out of heaven. Here I was, a kid who was passionate to learn everything I could about art—with so little opportunity in a small town up in the hills. And now a real artist was creating a real art studio next door to my house? It almost defied belief.

And not just any artist!

Glen Wessels had been head of the University of California art department for nearly thirty years. He founded the California College of Arts and Crafts, which is still training artists to this day. In the 1930s and through the war years, he lived among the intellectual expatriates in Paris, pursuing his artwork and spending endless hours in tiny, smoke-filled cafes with close friends such as Gertrude Stein, Pablo Picasso, and Ernest Hemingway.

Following the war, he returned to America, landed in Berkeley, and joined the university art department, ending up as its chair.

Glen was (and still is) one of my great heroes and mentors. He retired from active teaching at eighty, after his wife of fifty years died. She had been a concert pianist, and together they had traveled throughout Europe, cross-country skiing in the Alps.

In his later years, on a photographic trip in the California wilderness with legendary nature photographer Ansel Adams, Glen took a fall and ended up partially disabled. When I met him at his studio in the renovated barn, he was seventy-nine and had some difficulty getting around.

I became his legs for him; running errands, making purchases, cleaning the studio, and assisting in every way I could. In exchange, he taught me priceless lessons about painting—and life.

Glen viewed art as a priesthood, a calling higher than politics, higher than statesmanship. He believed an artist should be a true ambassador to the world. It was so contagious to me as a young teenager. I was over there every day, for two hours a day, and he would just talk to me as we worked together. I had the privilege of assisting Glen from age fourteen until—at his urging and with his blessing—I left home for college. That association became my single-minded focus through those years. I didn't want to go out for sports, I didn't want to write for the school newspaper, and I didn't have the vaguest idea of who might be taking whom to the junior-senior formal. None of that stuff mattered to me because my whole identity was in my painting, and in being Glen Wessels's apprentice.

I credit the high idealism reflected in all my art to that association with Glen. I'd already begun formulating some of those ideas in my mind during my years of working for Charlie Bell, but Glen helped me sharpen and refine them. Every painting I did I would show to Glen, and he would continue to affirm me and cast a vision before my eyes of pouring my life into art that would make a difference in people's lives.

A visionary love means putting yourself in your children's place.

Though Glen was an old man and crippled in body, he could still weave a powerful vision with his words. He showed me how I could actually live out what had only been boyhood fantasies.

I want to remember that lesson as a dad with four young daughters. Expressing my vision for each of them—out loud and in her hearing—is one of the most powerful, influential things I can do as a dad. A visionary love means putting yourself in your children's place and doing your best to understand their real desires, their awakening thoughts about how and where God might use them.

As parents, we need to cast that vision as widely as we can, dreaming and speculating out loud about where such interests, talents, and passions might lead.

Let's say you're talking to your young son about a few of his sketchy thoughts and notions about the future. Chances are, he's been thinking on a small scale. Stretch him a little. Help him to look wider and higher. Color in some of those faint pencil sketches with broad, bright strokes. After all, he may not be able to think much beyond the borders of your town or city. He may not realize that there is a whole world of opportunities out there. You can help him think outside the narrow fences of his limited experience and catch a glimpse of a wider world just waiting for him to employ his unique personality and God-given talents and abilities.

This is exactly what God does in my own life as a painter. He begins to sketch out radiant, light-filled visions in my mind...and then guides my hand as those visions take shape on an empty canvas.

I am loved by the Father with a visionary love, and I want to love my children in the same way.

*Therefore be
imitators of God,
as beloved children;
and walk in love,
just as Christ
also loved you....*

EPHESIANS 5:1–2, NASB

CHAPTER EIGHT

Playful Love

Thomas Kinkade

 Direct me in the path of your commands,
for there I find delight.

PSALM 119:35–36

I WOKE UP THIS MORNING WITH A STIFF NECK.

It feels for all the world as though I was in a major traffic accident yesterday—rear-ended at a stop sign by some tank of an SUV. But I know better. My pain has nothing to do with a fender bender.

It has everything to do with standing on my head.

You see, those aren't muscles that a middle-aged artist uses every day. In fact, I hadn't stood on my head since gym class in junior high. But I did last night. Twice. Nanette, too. In fact, everyone did but four-year-old Evie. She got to watch and laugh at the whole family. That's all right. Her time's coming!

Chalk it up to another uninhibited and unpredictable family night at the Kinkade hacienda. Yes, there are times when Dad and Mom fritter away some of their carefully cultivated reserve. But I'm convinced that we gain much, much more than we lose.

Children treasure the times when their parents get just a little bit silly, a little bit over-the-top. So

> *Children treasure the times when their parents get just a little bit silly, a little bit over-the-top.*

often, these are the memories that endure. Oh sure, in years to come the kids may remember the big trip to Yellowstone or the Statue of Liberty. They may recall the live symphony or the big-time tickets to the professional ball game. But chances are, the recollections that will cause the most smiles will be those wild'n'crazy moments…the pillow fights, the tickling wars, the practical jokes, the hilarious competitions and contests, the laughter over ridiculous jokes, and the uproarious family games.

Parents accustomed to functioning in a more staid, buttoned-down adult world need to set aside their inhibitions and polished image from time to time and enter the world of play—whether it be a duel over a Candy Land board or an interminable game of peek-a-boo with a toddler.

This is central to the Kinkade philosophy of parenting—and a very big part of any healthy family. The family that plays (not just prays) together stays together.

Just last night it was time for the two older ones to do the supper dishes. It's their job and responsibility, and they are well aware of it. But wouldn't you know it, I took a peek in the kitchen and there was Nanette, up to her elbows in dirty dishes, "helping" Chandler and Merritt.

"Nanette," I protested, "that's *their* job."

"I know, I know. But—I really want to help. It's a meaningful time to be with the girls, and we can talk as we work."

"Well, that's fine," I replied. "But I'm enough of a sexist to leave the job to you ladies. I've been working all day and I'm ready to put up my feet and relax—which is what you should be doing, too! I'm not going to be shamed into doing dishes and duplicating what I know *should* be the girls' job!"

Dodging a dish towel, I headed for the family room—a sunken area that serves as the principle Kinkade relaxation zone. My two little pals, Winsor and Evie, were still finishing their cookies at the dining room table. "C'mon girls," I called. "Finish up and let's get a game going."

They knew which game I meant. My little ones have learned how to play dominoes, and it's one of their current passions. As I pulled out the box, I suddenly wondered if they knew about stacking the dominoes in a long, long line—just for the pleasure of watching 'em fall. Could it be they'd never learned that this is one of the most fun things kids can do with dominoes?

In fact, it was a totally new concept for Winsor and Evie. They'd never heard or thought of stacking dominoes and couldn't wait to see how it worked.

That's one of the things I love so much about children. All the old games are brand new. All the ancient jokes, tired gags, riddles, and shticks are fresh material! Kids are just discovering life, ready for fun and adventure, love being silly and laughing, and haven't learned how to roll their eyes or become worldly-wise and cynical. When you think about it, what great companions they are! What fun little people are to hang out with!

As my brother and I were growing up, I don't think we ever learned how to play the real game of dominoes. For us, the whole object was to see how long a line we could achieve before we gave it the big push.

So the girls and I began to set up on our coffee table as Nanette came down to join us. "Hey girls," I said, "let's see if we can get the line to circle the whole table!"

After painstaking labor, we got about three-quarters of our way to the goal. Then Evie (I won't say whether by accident or on purpose) bumped one of the dominoes and set the whole thing off.

> *That's one of the things I love so much about children. All the old games are brand new.*

That gave us the idea of working in sections, leaving a temporary gap between each section. That way if someone (some anonymous, nameless little girl full of mischief and giggles) set off a chain reaction, it would only wipe out one section, not the whole enterprise. Finally, we got all of them lined up in a long, stately row encircling the table. Chandler came down from the kitchen, having finished her work, and got excited about what the little ones and I had constructed.

"Wow! That's cool. Let me see that. Can I be the one to knock it down?" (Could it be that a sixth grader hadn't seen dominoes in a row, either?)

"Sure," we said.

And down it went in beautiful symmetry, accompanied by the delighted shrieks of the little ones.

When it was time to start another game, I said, "Let's play war with the dominoes." That suggestion produced blank looks all around. "Oh, you know," I said, "we divide up the dominoes into stacks for each of us—with the dots facing down. Then each of us turns one over, and the highest number wins the hand—all four dominoes."

After that went on for a while, the fun began in earnest. I said, "Okay, whoever draws a zero—a blank domino—has to go stand on their head for one minute!"

> *I hadn't stood on my head since junior high school and wasn't sure I could pull it off.*

And that is how I acquired a stiff neck this morning. I pulled that zero! Right away! That wasn't how it was supposed to happen. I hadn't stood on my head since junior high school and wasn't sure I could pull it off. "Wait a minute," I protested, "I really don't think I can do this. Let's think of some other penalty."

"Oh no!" the girls shouted in unison. (I think Nanette sided with them, too.) "You HAVE to or it's no fair."

So I got down on the carpet for the headstand, with the girls cheering mightily. I don't think they'd ever seen their dad in that position before. After the deed was done, we went back to the table to draw again—and I had another bright idea. "Okay, *this* time whoever draws the double twelve (which is the number one domino) gets to be king and tell everybody else what to do."

So of course Evie, our four-year-old, drew the top domino.

"All right, Queen Evie," we said apprehensively, "what do we have to do?"

"*Everyone* gets to stand on their head!" she yelled.

So all of the queen's temporary subjects had a head-stand contest, and at least one of those subjects woke up with something akin to severe whiplash the next morning. But that's the fun of being playful and spontaneous as a family. You might end up with a few sore muscles or slightly bruised dignity—but you'll have some memories that will make it all worthwhile.

> You might end up with a few sore muscles or slightly bruised dignity—but you'll have some memories that will make it all worthwhile.

If you want to generate an irresistible magnetic force in your home that outdraws the appeal of the peer group, you really need such interludes. Your kids need to know that Mom and Dad know how to let loose, have some fun, and not be so serious all the time.

I've noticed that after my girls finish dinner, they seem to acquire a fresh charge of energy. More than anything else, I've observed, they seem to want to run around the house and scream. (In a house with boys, this might manifest itself in violent wrestling matches or an impromptu football game—with a roll of paper towels or some such item as the ball.)

Nanette and I have decided it would be counterproductive to stifle all that boiling, bubbling energy (as if we could), so we let them feel their oats and go wild for a time. And then again...sometimes we join in, too. We laugh. We yell. We chase each other around. It's an amazing stress reliever when you think about it. Maybe part of the problem with stuffy, uptight adults is they don't know how to "let go" of all that pent-up nervous energy. They need to take a silly pill from time to time, and just let themselves get down on their children's level.

Some of the most meaningful, bonding memories for kids come when you erase the dividing line between parent and child, if only for a few minutes.

You let down your guard.

You get drawn into a minor food fight.

You grab your pillow and go into battle.

You read a funny story and let yourself dissolve with laughter.

You launch a major water war with the garden hose.

Most any crazy thing that the kids will never forget is worth attempting. Some of the parents I talk to worry about "losing control" once they let their family cut loose a little. They fear they will somehow lose their authority if they let themselves become undignified or have too much fun.

We've never found it so at our house. In fact, when we need to pull it back in and get serious again, the transition occurs rather quickly. The girls know the boundaries and by and large respect them. If they don't respect the boundaries, then Nanette and I can quickly shift out of the playful mode and become the parents again.

MEMORIES OF LAUGHTER

The great thing about my mom when we were growing up was her ability to laugh. She would get absolutely hysterical laughing at my brother and me. I can't remember her getting down on a kid's level—playing games with us or being silly—but if Pat and I could get her laughing, look out! And just about anything went in our family humor.

> *Whatever else we were lacking in those days, we kept up a crazy, absurd humor that somehow knit us together.*

As teenagers, Pat and I were both pretty good-sized kids. And we thought it was hilarious how we could just tower over her. Mom would say to one of us, "Give me a hug." And we would reply, "No hug, Mom. But you're getting a dead lift." And we would sweep her off her feet and hold her above our heads like a barbell—while she squealed and laughed.

On Mom's eightieth birthday, just a few weeks ago, Pat and I were up in Placerville celebrating the big day with her. At one point she put her arms around Pat to give him a hug, and he said, "No hug, Mom. You're getting a dead lift."

"You wouldn't *dare*," she said, backing up slightly.

"Oh, yes I would," Pat replied.

And he did.

Humor was one of the things that kept our little family together, even in the face of the divorce and the single-parent home situation. Whatever else we were lacking in those days, we kept up a crazy, absurd humor that somehow knit us together. To this day, it is one of the foundations of my relationship with my mother, brother, and sister.

When my brother Pat and I were nine- and ten-year-olds, our dad began showing up for a couple of weeks each summer to take us on a trip. These were long, rambling journeys with no particular destination. We would just pile into the car, drive and drive, staying in cheap motels and eating in diners. We might end up in L.A., we might end up in Mexico—none of us really knew where we would end up. Nevertheless, it got us out of the house for a while through those long summer days and gave our mom a bit of a break.

I have one memory that stands out with unusual clarity. We were sitting around a motel room in Fresno one night in our underwear—nobody had any pajamas. And for whatever reason, it suddenly struck Pat and me funny that Dad was sitting there in his shorts watching TV. We started to laugh at him.

"Hey," he said. "What's up with you guys?"

"Oh, Dad," we said, "you just look so funny sitting there in your boxers."

Like a shot, he jumped up off the edge of the bed.

"You think *that's* funny?" he said. "How about this?" Immediately, he went into a vaudeville soft-shoe routine, shuffling around the room in his underwear with an imaginary cane and top hat, singing "Me and My Shadow." That sent Pat and me rolling onto the floor, laughing until our sides ached.

Believe it or not, that became one of the most vividly etched memories of my times with Dad. We never did have very much time with him, and he wasn't around for us when we needed and wanted a father.

But say what you will, on a hot night in a cheap motel in Fresno, he made us laugh like we'd never laughed before. And that, at least, counts for something.

As parents, we concern ourselves with the negative influences, the harmful peer groups, and the undesirable companions in the lives of our growing children. And we do well to be concerned about those things. But in the long run, we'll face a losing battle if we haven't made our own homes into relaxed, happy, accepting, sometimes hilarious havens that make kids really *want* to be there.

Have you ever noticed the brightly lit windows in one of my paintings—the warm glow of cozy radiance pouring out into the shadowy twilight? I like to think there is laughter behind that welcoming light...parents and children who love being together and know how to have fun as a family.

And by the way, if you get close enough to peek through one of those windows, you just might catch a glimpse of someone old enough to know better...trying to stand on his head.

A

CHAPTER NINE

Releasing Love

I have no greater joy than to hear
that my children are walking in the truth.

3 JOHN 1:4

IT'S A DANCE.

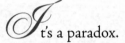

Our children grow away from us— even as they root ever deeper in the soil of our hearts.

It's a paradox.

It's a long tightrope walk in the dark.

It's holding on as you let go.

It's stepping back as you stand ready to step in.

It's knowing when to offer a word of counsel, and when to keep silent, allowing circumstances and consequences to speak for themselves.

It's hearing the call for freedom, and recognizing the silent cry for security and stability.

It's balancing three or four resolute no's with one strategic yes.

Every day of their lives, our children grow away from us—even as they root ever deeper in the soil of our hearts. A father's job is to shelter and protect his children and at the same time prepare them to stand on their own. A mother's task is to nurture her sons and daughters, even as she shows them how to make a home out in the wider world.

How do you do that? How do you draw your children close while you're in the very act of giving them wings? It will never be an easy task and—because of the inevitable tension involved—it won't win moms and dads many popularity contests. Ultimately, you are your child's *parent*—not a friend or buddy.

Even though our eventual goal is "letting go," we limit our children's decisions until they're ready for independence. We don't allow them to run their own lives until they've demonstrated the capacity to stand alone.

That time may coincide with an eighteenth birthday, or it may not. The key is not chronological age, but true maturity.

Today, for two hours, Merritt will breathe the heady air of new freedom.

Her senior lifeguard course at the swim and tennis club lasts until noon. At two, I'll pick her up when I bring Winsor and Evie in for swim lessons. She will meet with friends for lunch and stay there and play tennis until I arrive with the little ones.

This is new territory for a Kinkade girl. She has free, unsupervised time. She has possession (temporarily) of the family cell phone. She's having lunch with her pals at a restaurant. The prospect of this brief solo flight was *so* exciting to her this morning. She feels more "on her own" than ever before.

We'll see how she does. Frankly, I'm hoping for the best but reserving judgment. Our family policy says that you earn your privileges. As you handle each situation properly and maturely, then maybe next time the tether goes out just a little bit further. But if she were to abuse the cell phone, or didn't show up at our scheduled meeting place on time, then we'd have to hold back on those privileges for a while.

Merritt, however, is highly motivated to earn more independence. Every time we schedule a meeting time or place, she's there with two minutes to spare—just to make sure she isn't late. She's doing her best to demonstrate that she's ready to try her wings a little, so that next time she might fly a little further and higher. I've got a feeling today's experiment with freedom will go very well. You can count on the fact that the three younger girls will be watching! Merritt's out there blazing the trail that one day they hope to follow.

> *How do you draw your children close while you're in the very act of giving them wings?*

Thomas and I believe that "letting go" needs to be a very gradual process. When Merritt was learning to walk, we started by holding both of her little hands as those chubby legs churned along beneath her. Before long, she only needed to grasp a single, guiding index finger to keep her balance. And then what? Did we say, "You're on your own now, sweetie"? No, we walked alongside her, ready to lend a balancing hand if needed. A little later, we stood ready to welcome her with wide open arms at the end of a ten-foot solo walk across the family room.

This is yet another "solo walk" for Merritt. Another in a series of many...

...before that day when she walks up onto a platform at high school graduation.

...before that day when she walks away from the family car toward a dorm room at college.

...before that day when she walks down an aisle to meet a young man standing at the altar.

And even then, if the Lord leaves Thomas and me here on earth, we'll be there to cheer her on. We'll be there to offer a guiding, balancing hand if she needs it. We'll be there to open our arms and pour out our love and affirmation for every accomplishment, or in the disappointment of failure and loss. She's our girl, and she always will be.

> *"Letting go" needs to be a very gradual process.*

Every day, growing children show their parents what they're capable of. And with Merritt at age fourteen, it's basically up to her to show us what privileges she can handle.

We'll give her all the freedom that will bless her and help her.

We'll withhold the freedom that would expose her to danger and lasting hurt or would compromise our family unity.

God has given us that tightrope, and we need to walk its length every day in His strength and wisdom. He *is* our balance; we would be foolish to rely on our own. 🐚

Each one of us, as we mature, needs to learn how to make decisions for ourselves, and also how to accept the inevitable consequences of those choices. As our girls begin to make such decisions—whether Merritt at fourteen or Winsor at seven—Nanette and I want to be there for them, offering whatever resources we have.

We offer them the resource of simply *being there*, focused and aware, when they need our attention.

We offer them the resource of a happy, stable home. A home where they are accepted and affirmed for who they are, not for what they might achieve.

We offer them the resource of our wisdom—wisdom from the Lord, and hard-won knowledge from our collective experiences through the years.

We offer them the resource of unconditional love—our open arms, listening ear, and compassion when they make unwise choices and experience the painful results.

What a balancing act parents face!

But it's never easy with growing kids because the scene is constantly changing. (Remember the kaleidoscope?) When do you exercise control and when do you dial it back? When do you shelter and when do you release? When do you draw a hard line in the sand and when do you admit that the line never belonged there in the first place?

I know this: We won't be able to adopt a cookie-cutter approach with our four girls. Each of our daughters is her own person, and each will face the challenges of life through a different set of eyes, a different walk with Christ, and a different level of maturity. Yes, the girls will constantly compare "what-you-let-so-and-so-do-when-she-was-this-age." Siblings have engaged in that activity since Adam and Eve were with family. But Nanette and I will be watching for signs of emerging maturity and responsibility rather than watching the calendar.

I had lunch with my friend Pat a few days ago, and we found ourselves talking about these very things. That's not so surprising, I suppose, when you realize that he too has four daughters. But the difference lies in the fact that his daughters are now grown, with homes of their own, while ours are very much in the nest.

As we talked, Pat seemed a little melancholy. Looking back, he wishes he hadn't been quite so controlling, quite so strict with those lovely young ladies. He wanted their respect, he knew what was right, but now he's thinking he was just too inflexible—*especially in areas where a little bend and give wouldn't have hurt anything at all.* He wonders if he has created some lingering hurt and unhappy memories in his daughters' hearts over this more heavy-handed approach.

My friend tends to be a little hard on himself. His daughters love their dad and are doing very well in life. But what a balancing act parents face! You're out there on that slender tightrope with a thousand distractions and wind gusts from three directions. Pat is already across that rope, on the other side looking back. But Nanette and I are still "out there" over empty space—we're on the spot, on the line—stepping ever so carefully, day by day, seeking to maintain a balance that will see us through.

As we've discussed these things through the years (recognizing that parenting is more subjective art than precise science), Nanette and I believe that we can hold firm on issues pertaining

to morality and the family…but give leeway on matters of individuality and style. As I've said, our four girls are as different from one another as can be. And we want to allow them to be themselves—to stake out the turf of their individuality and feel good about that. We want to give them the freedom to make some choices—in areas that are not consequential to their moral lives or their personal futures—recognizing that those choices could be very different from the ones Nanette and I might make.

> *We want to allow them to stake out the turf of their individuality.*

As we mentioned, Merritt wore overalls until she turned thirteen. Nanette and I would have loved to see her dress in more attractive, feminine things. And there were certainly those occasions when we insisted on it. Most of the time, however, we let Merritt express her individuality. At that point in her life, she was all tomboy and denim. And then, wonder of wonders, at age thirteen she fell in love with pretty, feminine attire. And it was *her* idea!

We're learning that if we push noncritical issues and areas of our personal preference, we may win those smaller battles…but possibly lose some much bigger ones later on. Through sometimes difficult experience, we're learning to trust God on some of those less crucial issues, and we find that most of the time the kids will "come around" to a different point of view without too much meddling on our part.

Our job as parents is to lead our children into certain basic values—values that will keep them and protect them and bless them for the rest of their lives, even after we've gone on. We must hold firm to those values, even as we allow our sons and daughters to explore and grow and express themselves in a host of ways. Kids need to step up to the plate in areas of responsibility, work ethic, personal achievement, and—if they're so inclined—sports performance. My girls need to stand on their own in these areas and mature through trial and error, success and setback.

> *Behavior patterns set in the teen years may very well follow them the rest of their lives.*

But I don't believe for a minute that the same latitude applies to areas of moral compromise or threats to family togetherness. We would no more allow our eleven-year-old and fourteen-year-old to set their own hours or social agenda than we would allow the two little ones to set their own menus or bedtime.

I've heard parents say, "Well, if my daughter wants to hang out at the mall all day, I guess she's old enough to make that decision for herself."

Not necessarily! In fact, parents need to be even more vigilant and protective of their teenagers than when the children were preteens or toddlers. The dangers are every bit as real. The consequences of wrong decisions loom larger than ever. Behavior patterns set in the teen years may very well follow them the rest of their lives.

So we draw lines in our family. We remain firm when we need to be, even in the face of protests and tears and lawyerly arguments. But we always look for ways to say yes—especially on issues that seem monumentally important to the kids.

In our family, togetherness is what we would call a watershed issue. We believe in doing everything we can to make the family so fun, so engaging, so affirming, that the peer group will lose much of its magnetic drawing power.

So when the whole family went to the orientation meeting for Merritt's new high school, we naturally expected her to sit with us.

I even went so far to make it an issue with Nanette before we left. "By jiminy, I know most of those kids will want to sit with other kids instead of being with their families. But I want Merritt with us. It's a family experience, and she belongs with us."

For whatever reason, I was getting myself worked up before the issue was even an issue. Nanette simply maintained a diplomatic silence.

Merritt had a soccer game first, and we planned to meet her at the high school. When we arrived (wouldn't you know it), there she was, sitting in one of the front rows with half a dozen nervous freshmen girls. She had already made some new friends, and they looked as cute as they could be, sitting huddled together in a single row like a flock of sparrows on a telephone line.

When Nanette saw them, she said, "Oh, Thom, can't she just sit up there with her friends?"

"No," I said, sounding more insistent than I felt. "She needs to sit with her family. We already made that decision. We told her she could go to the soccer game with her friends, but that she was going to sit with us when we got here."

Father has spoken!

And then Merritt came over to us, her eyes full of pleading.

"Please, Dad," she whispered, "can't I sit with my friends? *Please?* No one is sitting with their family. Can't I stay with my friends?"

Time slowed down in those few seconds before I answered. Somehow, in several rapid blinks of the eye, I did a lot of thinking. How would I have felt at that age, sitting with my mother when all my pals were sitting together? Here she was, in a scary new situation, and she wanted the support and encouragement of being surrounded with other girls who were going through the same thing. They all felt the newness, the strangeness, the awkwardness, and Merritt was drawing strength from the shared experience.

How unreasonable was that?

In fact, it wasn't unreasonable at all.

I climbed down off my rigid position (avoiding Nanette's eyes), and gave her the thumbs up to return to her schoolmates in the front row. And what happened as a result? She loved sitting with her friends, and then right after the program was over, she came back to the family and stuck with us like glue for the rest of the evening. We explored the campus together, met some of the families, and had a happy, relaxed evening.

Had I drawn a hard inflexible line that night, I certainly could have won that battle…but what would I have won? A little solace to my pride? Maybe. But how much emotional, relational capital would I have invested on a issue that didn't really matter that much? How might I have weakened our position as parents for standing firm on those issues that truly are nonnegotiable?

> *A few well-considered yes's on less weighty issues keep kids in the game.*

On that night, one small item got removed from that Personal List of Desired Freedoms that every teen carries in his or her hip pocket. Nanette and I are very aware that if that list gets too long, with no hint or hope of fulfillment on any front, it may eventually lead to complete discouragement—or even outright rebellion. There are plenty of teens out there ready to jump into a discussion about how unreasonable and dictatorial their parents are.

Save up your parental ammunition for those inevitable moral battles, when you will have to say no and make it stick. A few well-considered yes's on less weighty issues keep kids in the game.

They'll be less inclined to write off their parents as complete tyrants or ogres. And if home remains a fun, adventurous, and accepting place, they'll be more inclined to stay linked to the people with the same last name.

Releasing—or being released, for that matter—can be a frightening part of life. But when it all takes place in the context of warmth and love and indomitable togetherness, those brief solo journeys into freedom and independence lose much of their terror...and take on a glow of joy.

When our children reach up for a balancing hand, Nanette and I will be there for them. And when we as parents feel the earth lurch beneath us, we'll reach up a hand, too.

Our Father will be there for us. Just like always.

Do not fear,
for I am with you;
do not be dismayed,
for I am your God.
I will strengthen
you and help you;
I will uphold you with
my righteous right hand.

ISAIAH 41:10

A Love

CHAPTER TEN

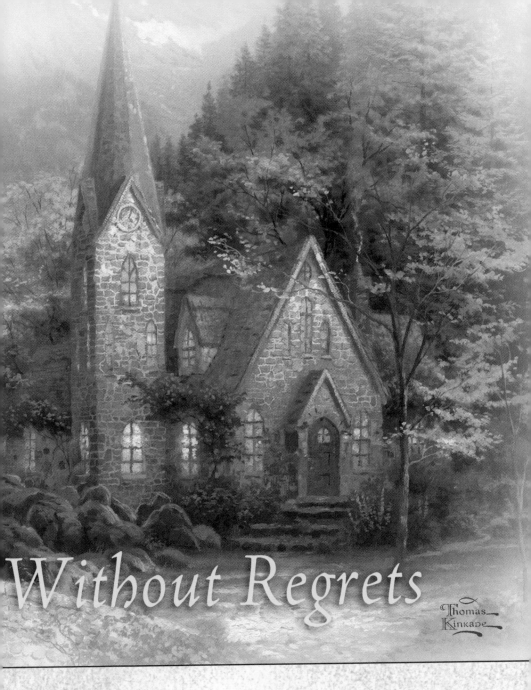

Without Regrets

Thomas Kinkade

 will never fail you.

I will never forsake you.

HEBREWS 13:5, NLT

A LOVE WITHOUT REGRETS ON SOME FUTURE DAY MEANS CONSISTENCY— AND A LITTLE TOUGH LOVE—TODAY.

It may mean holding the line on some very difficult issues.

It may mean saying no when everything in you wants to say yes.

It may mean losing some points with your kids today, in the hope of gaining those points back, with interest, on a distant tomorrow.

It will certainly mean doing the best you know how with the information and resources and wisdom you have at hand, and humbly leaning hard on God through every bit of it.

Our girls understand that our home is different. They may not always celebrate that fact, they may not even appreciate that fact. But they understand it. They know that the Kinkades have a family identity uniquely our own. We don't always do things the way their friends' families do things, and we refuse to be drawn into the comparison game. It's not go-with-the-flow at our house

"But all the kids get to do this! Why can't we?"

158

because Nanette and I don't believe in passive parenting.

We believe in disciplining our children, but thankfully, I'm not called on to exercise it very often. The girls—especially the older ones—are just so in tune with who we are as a family and have such an identity in the Lord that many of those so-called inevitable conflicts never gain much traction.

It's not a situation where the kids would assume, "Well, all my friends went to such-and-such movie, so it's probably okay for me to go to that movie."

It's not even in the cards! The girls understand our family's way of doing things. We have foundational values. We live by standards, and there are consequences for inappropriate behavior.

As I said, my daughters don't always like that. From time to time, they may even hit us with that age-old comeback, "But *all* the kids get to do this! Why can't we?" And I will usually reply, "We're the Kinkades. This is the way *we* do it. Aren't you proud to be in a family that really cares about these things?"

I mentioned my friend, Pat, who maintained some rather strict rules in his Hollywood home. He reflected that several of his daughters' friends liked to hang out with his family, in part *because* of those standards and that structure. In their own homes, it was "anything goes." Boyfriends in the bedrooms? No problem. Alcohol? Drugs? Why not?

These kids longed for the security of a home with walls that didn't move, a foundation that didn't shift, and a dad and mom who kissed their kids good-night and locked the doors.

On several occasions recently, I've overheard Merritt tell her friends, "Oh, in our family we're not allowed to go to the mall unless a parent is there." Or, "In our family, we don't watch TV. We *do* things together."

I hear an element of family identity in those words, and it makes me glad. Holding to family standards can truly be taught as a positive. *Our family is different. Our family always does it this way.* And we can take pride in our uniqueness.

And yet...having said all that, we go all out to make this the most fun, adventurous, accepting, responding, secure place to grow up that we possibly can. Nanette and I pour ourselves into making contact, planning trips, and giving the children all the time and energy and attention we can muster.

Some might call that sacrificial, but we really can't imagine living in any other way. Building a strong, happy marriage and family pays off every day of our lives—and holds the promise of peace and sharing and laughter for years to come.

Let me urge you in this last chapter: Go against the grain of our "me" culture, and give yourself away for your family. Affirm, discipline, model, listen, hug, and reach out in every way you know how. Do all you can to build family identity, family fun, family ties, and family traditions. If you do, you just may discover that your daughters and sons really don't want to rebel or escape from your home at first opportunity.

In fact, there is nowhere they would rather be.

Nanette: ॐ

     *T*homas and I just got back from a little time away together at Lake Tahoe—a spot we've loved since our courting days. It was one of those slower, quieter vacations, with ample time to reflect on our priorities as a couple and the truly important things of life.

Mostly, we thought about our blessings.

The Lord tells us in Scripture that we *will* have trouble in this world, and our family is no exception. We certainly don't expect immunity from hardships and trials. Yet for the moment, in this brief season of our lives, the winds have been gentle, with lots of warm sunshine. He has been so very, very kind to us. When you have your health, your family, and the Lord, you really have everything. You have something that the whole world is looking for, but can never seem to find....

Happiness.

It is too precious a gift to take for granted, barter for some lesser thing, or fritter away through neglect. Out there by that lovely blue lake (Mark Twain called it a "beautiful relic of fairy-land forgotten"), we made a fresh commitment to each other. We promised never to allow the pressures of business to detract from our relationship with our children, with each other, and with the Lord.

We don't want to look back with regret on these few fleeting years with our girls. Maybe our business will continue to thrive, and maybe it won't. Maybe the Kinkades will enjoy times of prosperity and plenty, or maybe times will become very lean, as they were when we were first married.

Hardly any of us will reach old age without bruises and a few lingering sorrows. It comes with the territory of our fallible human lives. But God helping us, there are certain pangs we never want to experience: We don't want to look back on a fractured marriage or a broken family.

On some future day, sitting by the fire…strolling by the lake…or watching leaves fall outside an autumn window…we will say to one another, "We may have made a lot of mistakes, but we took the time to be a couple, and we took the time to be a family. We loved each other with all our hearts, and we were there, on the scene, when our girls needed us."

> *Do all you can to build family identity, family fun, family ties, and family traditions.*

And if I ever find myself daydreaming about "what might have been," or what I might have accomplished in some career "out there," or where I wished I had gone or what I wished I had done, I hope I have the grace to stop myself. I hope I have the presence of mind to say, *What more could you have wanted, Nanette Kinkade? You were a wife and you were a mother. You made your home a secure, loving shelter from the darkness and sorrows of the* world. You were there for your kids when they needed a mom.

What more are people looking for? What else is out there that could bring such satisfaction or fulfillment?

That's what Thomas and I are trying to achieve. We just want to do the best we can, with God's help, so that we can look back without regrets. We want to be able to say, "You know, maybe we weren't perfect parents, and maybe some of our attitudes or ideas were a little skewed, but we sure did love those kids."

For us, the family is the very heart of everything we strive for. We could accomplish a great many things, and certainly Thomas has been blessed with amazing opportunities to make a difference in this world. But if we've missed caring for our marriage and family, we are off target in a tragic, irredeemable way.

Looking down the road, of course, is one thing. Daily life is something else! There are times, as a mom, when I feel overwhelmed by the needs and demands of raising four young girls. The pressure seems so unrelenting on some days. Every now and then, when the anxiety runs high, I wonder if I'll be able to handle it.

Somewhere in the midst of it all, I'm reminded of a simple truth: Life is made up of seasons. God is well aware of the days of our lives and knows when we're enduring a difficult passage. That's why He says, "I will never fail you. I will never forsake you." And that Bible passage goes on to say, "The Lord is my helper, so I will not be afraid" (Hebrews 13:5–6, NLT).

> *For us, the family is the very heart of everything we strive for.*

God will give us grace for those days of distress and bewilderment...and then it will get better. It truly will. The difficult days will pass, life will change again, and you'll exchange one set of blessings and challenges for another. It's not as though there will never be any relief from the ordeal or heartache you are experiencing on one particular day or week of your life. In time, you will leave that era and move into another. You may find the peace and rest you've been hoping for, or you may find yourself facing some new challenge. Either way, God is sufficient for your needs. Either way, you will move on. That's the way life works.

As I write these words, we still have little ones running around the house, with their squeals and giggles, their mischief, tenderness, and tears. And I know that—no matter how I might feel on any given day—I will miss this season when it's gone. I'm doing my best to relish the sweet times, the fun times, and bear in mind that the challenging aspects will change.

> *We want to embrace this time and value it as the gift from God that it truly is.*

Right now we're in such a heavenly phase. In many ways, it's the summer of our lives. Thomas and I have been married twenty years, all the kids are still in the nest, and we're treasuring up memory after memory. We want to embrace this time and value it as the gift from God that it truly is.

It won't always be this way.

It may not be this way very long.

But while we're in the middle of it, we refuse to be distracted. We're going to thank God for it and savor it.

I know that with two-income families time is always at a premium. But I've always believed you can make time for anything that you feel is a big enough priority. Outside of your relationship with God and your spouse, I can't think of a higher priority than connecting with your children. In reality, the blessing of that contact goes both ways. Not only will your child be empowered from that together time, but so will you! It's one of those situations where the more you give, the more you will benefit and receive from the relationship (in the long haul). You'll be building memories to ponder years and years from now.

Maybe you can't spend focused time every day—or even every week—with each of your children. Maybe it has to be a once-a-month date. Or maybe you'll find a way to wedge it in a lunch break, picking up one of the kids at school and going out for a quick burger or a taco.

You might have to improvise.

You might have to be creative.

You might have to squeeze your calendar.

You might have to inconvenience yourself, or give up something you'd rather do. Even so, you *can* do it. You can find the time. You can make a way. You can push it, link by link, up the priority chain.

If you want to. 🐚

I love perfect moments, in perfect worlds.

I like to paint landscapes where the fall of humanity has never cast its shadow.

...Where the snow is white and pristine, and light and laughter (and a mug of hot cocoa) wait just inside the frosty windows.

...Where a summer rain has kissed the morning streets, awakening the fragrance of flowers and newly cut lawns, and then passed on before the sun crests the horizon.

...Where the afternoon thunderheads roll back from the mountains just in time to catch a regal sunset.

...Where smoke wafts from the chimney of a cottage beside the

stream, and the footpath winding into the distance promises adventure, beauty, and tranquil joy.

A piece of art, after all, is a compact form of the universe. I try to make that world comfortable and understandable. In all of my landscapes, I invite the viewer to imagine a life where there is plenty of time, plenty of energy, plenty of opportunity for everything you feel is important—plus a little leftover for some things you simply enjoy.

But life isn't always like that, is it?

We live in a fallen world, where the rain is wet, the snow is cold, and promising pathways might end at a locked gate, or the edge of a canyon. Marriages don't always live up to the deepest longings of those who stand together at the altar and pledge their lives to one another. Children don't always follow their parents along the best and wisest of trails, but turn in their own directions, walking in desolate places and shadow.

> *Outside of your relationship with God and your spouse, I can't think of a higher priority than connecting with your children.*

Nanette and I have known hard times and times of abundance. As both husband and wife, father and mother, we have experienced our share of pressure, disappointment, and stress. Because of all the ups and downs, because of the strains and worries and changed expectations, we might have been pulled apart. We might have been one more couple that called it quits and went our separate ways...one more family unraveling in the wind and drifting apart.

It doesn't have to happen that way. While there are no guarantees, there are priorities we can all pursue that will make a lasting difference. By giving your whole heart to the precedence of building and maintaining your marriage and family relationships, and (most of all) by tapping into the resources and power of a loving God, you can create your own small world of fragrance and light.

It isn't a fairy tale, or the misty dreams of a romantic, idealistic painter. It's a possibility as real as tomorrow's sunrise.

Yes, it takes long, hard, deliberate effort. And no, it may not be easy. It may not happen all at once. It may not even be realized for years. It will certainly come with a price tag.

And it won't happen without bucketfuls of grace and forgiveness...between husband and wife...between parents and children...between brothers and sisters. Most of all, we need the grace of God to cover our failures and sins and to heal all wounds, whether surface or deep, whether old or new.

Without grace, we would quickly run out of hope.

In Jesus Christ, we needn't run out of either.

ART INDEX